The Pocket Gillie

FLYFISHING ESSENTIALS

Scott Richmond

Drawings by Lora Creswick

FOUR RIVERS PRESS
WEST LINN, OREGON

Acknowledgments

Lora Creswick for the line drawings; give the cat a growl for me. Dan Casali for layout and for suggesting the original concept and title; you may have gotten me into this but I'll still be your friend. John Laursen for book and cover design; thanks for helping the aesthetically-impaired. Dennis Cunningham for the cover art. Dr. Norman Anderson for entomology help. Madelynne Diness for editing and advice. Jim Schollmeyer for photographing flies. Randall Kaufmann for advice and for supplying the flies for the photos. Frank Amato for advice. Randy Stetzer, John Hazel, and Rod Robinson for review. William Shakespeare for quotations from his plays. My wife Barbara for keeping cool.

Four Rivers Press, Inc.
19996 South Sweetbriar Road
West Linn, Oregon 97068

Printed in the United States of America

10 9 8 7 6 5 4 3 2 1

Contents

ONE

Introduction

In Scotland and Ireland, where many fly fishing traditions developed, a gillie is a fishing guide. He knows the water and its inhabitants intimately, and stands by the angler giving advice on where the best fish are, which fly to use, and how to present it.

This book will serve as such a guide for you. It is a collection of practical, bread-and-butter facts and techniques that you will find useful while on the water. There are many excellent books on fly fishing suitable for reading in your living room, but this book is to be used while you are waist deep in a river, or bobbing about a lake in your float tube. It is your pocket guide—a gillie in your pocket—ready to offer advice on what to do.

How to Use This Book

I am for all waters.
   Twelfth Night

Basic Decisions

There are three basic decisions to make in fly fishing. They are, in the order in which they should be made:

1. *Where to fish* (where to present)

2. *Which fly to use* (what to present)

3. *Which presentation is best for the fly you choose,* in the place you have chosen to fish it (how to present)

Chapters 2 and 3 of this book cover the essential information you need to help you with these decisions.

There are basic preparations needed before going fishing; these are detailed in this chapter. General information about aquatic insects is found in Chapter 4, while Chapter 5 covers identification of insects. There are also some miscellaneous subjects; these are in Chapter 6. There is a glossary at the end of Chapter 6.

Generalizations — Uses and Abuses

In order to be useful this book presents generalizations about many aspects of fly fishing, particularly aquatic entomology. Thus about 80% of fly fishing situations are covered in a book that can be carried in your vest. Covering the exceptions to the generalizations would result in a book you couldn't carry in a pickup truck.

Generalizations are useful to the angler because they allow simplification and provide a framework for thought and action. The danger is in letting the generalizations become rigid limits to both creative thought and the recognition of exceptions. The angler needs to recognize when a generalization is failing, and then seek a solution to the exception.

Lakes and Rivers

This book refers often to "lakes" and "rivers," meaning by these terms "still water" and "moving water," respectively. If you fish both kinds of water very much you find that the distinctions can blur. Portions of some rivers are so slow moving that they have aquatic life usually associated with lakes, and the fishing tactics should change to those for lakes. Conversely, parts of some lakes act like rivers. Anglers need to be alert and ready to change their tactics as needed.

How Not to Use This Book

Although the author is naturally pedantic, this book is not intended to be used as a primer on fly fishing. On the other hand, it can be a handy reference when reading other fly fishing books.

The Three Never-Fail Rules of Fly Fishing

There are no rules that guarantee successful fly fishing. There is no perfect fly that will always induce a rise, no sure-fire presentation that will always entice a fish, no fool-proof method for locating big fish ready to take the fly. The author has found only three invariable and infallible rules, which are offered here.

Rule 1: *You should always listen to the experts, but you shouldn't always believe them.*

Rule 2: *Some people's advice should never be followed.*

Rule 3: *In any given body of water, on any given day, there exists one really dumb fish that will confidently accept anything presented to it in any manner.*

Corollary to Rule 3: *There is no relationship between the size of the fish and the stupidity of the angler's technique.*

Rule 3 is a versatile rule. When an angler applies it to himself, it keeps him from taking himself too seriously. The astute angler will notice, however, that when Rule 3 is applied to other people it helps explain away their success. Thus contemplating Rule 3 not only keeps the angler humble, it provides comfort when others are catching more fish. This is a useful rule indeed.

Preparation Before Going Fishing

Things to Do Before You Leave

Refer to a fishing guidebook. Good ones have a wealth of information concisely presented.

Talk to someone at a fly shop, preferably one that is close to your destination. Ask them about hatches, what flies to bring, best places and times of day to fish, and other local knowledge. Sometimes fly shops will have a hatch table for local waters. Local knowledge can be extremely useful, but see Rule 1 in the previous section first.

Check your checklist. Checklists are individual things, but a few ideas about what you might bring are listed below.

    ___This book
    ___Vest
    ___Rod (its amazing what people will forget)
    ___Reels and spare spools
    ___Waders
    ___Wading boots
    ___Wading staff
    ___Wader patching kit
    ___Float tube and fins
    ___License and other permits
    ___Net
    ___Flies suitable for destination, as well as alternative
        destinations
    ___Spare leaders
    ___Tippet material
    ___Nymph indicators
    ___Line dressing

___Dry fly floatant
___Leader sink
___Lead (make sure it can be easily removed from the leader)
___Rubber for straightening leader
___Hook hone
___Nippers
___Knife
___Forceps
___Collection and identification kit:
    ___nymph net
    ___ruler
    ___collection vials
    ___hand lens
    ___tweezers
    ___white lid
___Thermometer
___Monocular or binoculars
___Polarizing sunglasses
___Rain gear
___Hat
___Gloves
___Sunscreen
___Bug repellent
___Gas money
___Flashlight
___Water
___Food/snacks
___Camera and film
___Streamside fly tying kit
___First-aid kit
___Snake bite kit

Make sure you have flies that are appropriate for where you are going, and for the time of year. Also, carry flies that are suited to alternate locations that you might go to if your primary destination in not fishable.

Get a good map. Topographical maps—ones showing elevation contours—can help you pinpoint the location of cliffs, inlet streams, and other key features. They can also keep you from getting hopelessly lost.

Know what species of fish to expect. Different trout species behave differently. Knowing what to expect helps you choose the best tactics.

Check the regulations. They may have changed since the last time you went there.

Check the weather forecast. Expect worse weather than is predicted, and pack clothing accordingly. A valuable item to have in your gear bag is a weather radio. These nifty gadgets are available in most electronics stores, and allow you to receive 24 hour broadcasts from the National Weather Service.

Check streamflow and gauging data. This information is often available from public agencies or power companies that own dams. Reservoir levels are often available, too. Changes in water level and streamflow can drastically impact the fishing on both lakes and rivers.

Advice to Beginners

If you are a beginning flyfisher, your eyes may glaze over when you look at certain portions of this book. "Do I really need to know all this stuff?" you may ask. No, you don't; at least, not yet. A beginning or occasional flyfisher will do better by concentrating on a few basic skills and doing them well. Read through the entire book so you know what's in it and where to find it, then focus on the skills listed below.

Learn to recognize trout resting places, and food production and concentration zones. That way you won't spend your time fishing over unproductive water. It's not necessary to know all the possibilities. Learn to recognize three or four key ones that apply to the water you fish the most. (Chapter 2)

You can get by with just two kinds of casts: overhead and roll. Learn to cast distances of 5 to 40 feet with consistent accuracy; 90% of fishing situations can be handled with casts of this distance. (Chapter 6)

There are four presentations for rivers you should know: upstream dry, upstream emerger, deep nymph with indicator, and wet fly swing. (Chapter 3)

If you fish lakes, you can get by with two presentations: count-down-and-retrieve, and slow retrieve.(Chapter 3)

Understand the Points of Vulnerability (POV) concept and observe it in action when trout are feeding. (Chapter 3)

Learn to use the POV charts. Ask other people (such as at your local fly shop) what insects to expect where you are going, then look them up in the chart. (Chapter 3)

Understand the different styles of flies and how they relate to POV. (Chapter 3)

Learn to distinguish aquatic insect orders so you know if you are looking at a mayfly, caddisfly, stonefly, midge, dragonfly, or damselfly. Learn this for both adult and pre-adult forms. Later, as you get more experienced, you can learn finer differentiations — but start with the basics. (Chapters 4,5)

Read the section on wading, and be careful. (Chapter 6)

Understand leader basics. Leaders are very important. (Chapter 6)

Understand mending and other ways of dealing with drag. (Chapter 6)

Learn how to release trout unharmed. (Chapter 6)

There are five knots you should know: improved surgeons, blood, double turle, improved clinch, and nail. Practice these knots so you can tie them easily. When the light is fading and fish are rising, you will want to be able to tie good knots quickly. (Chapter 6)

Develop good observation skills so you can recognize changes in the aquatic environment.

Understand the ethics and etiquette of fly fishing. (Chapter 6)

Cultivate an attitude of curiosity about the fishing environment, and care about its preservation and enhancement.

The five biggest problems that beginning flyfishers have are:
    Finding productive water
    Casting
    Managing slack line
    Getting a drag-free drift
    Knots

TWO

Finding the Trout

Trout are simple creatures and are always thinking about one of four things:

Eating
A safe life, with little hard work or risk
Spawning
Nothing

They are a lot like your cousin Fred, except fish only think about spawning once a year. And, as with Fred, you have little influence over trout's behavior in the latter two cases, so concentrate on the former. You will find trout in places with food, or in safe places where they can rest easily, or—most commonly—in safe resting places near food.

The next four sections describe common resting and feeding places in rivers and lakes. The remainder of the chapter discusses how to use your observations of these to find concentrations of fish, and to locate big trout. The chapter concludes with some guidelines for visually locating fish.

Resting Places in Rivers

In rivers, trout will seek havens from their predators and relief from the current. To elude airborne predators (eagles, osprey, etc.) trout look for overhead cover or depth. To avoid aquatic predators (otters, other fish) they head for hiding places such as boulder fields.

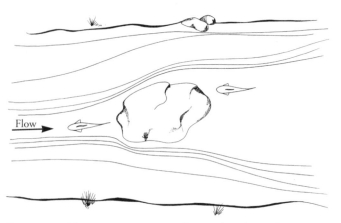

Figure 2-1. *Obstructions create resting places, such as this midstream boulder with quiet water behind and in front. Because current is diverted away from the boulder, the quiet water behind it is wider than the boulder.*

When the water is very warm there is another criteria for a good resting place: oxygen. Oxygen dissolves in water in inverse proportion to the water's temperature, so warmer water holds less oxygen. When the water is warm trout will seek areas with more oxygen, such as riffles, inlet streams, springs, and deep pools.

The other side of the temperature equation is very cold water. In extreme weather, and when available, trout may gather around geothermal springs to keep warm.

The resting places shown below meet one or more of these criteria. The criteria that are met are indicated as follows:

Relief from current   (R)

Safety from predators   (S)

Oxygen   (O)

Warmth   (W)

Resting Places

Downstream from obstructions, such as boulders, logs, bridge abutments. **(R)**

Immediately upstream from obstructions, as well as to the sides, and in between obstructions. **(R)**

Immediately downstream from a point that juts into the river. **(R)**

In deeper water just upstream from an area that gets shallow. For example, in a tailout. Usually trout will not move into these areas until dawn or dusk. If found there at other times of day they tend to be wary. **(R)**

Figure 2-2. *A point of land creates quiet water downstream from it.*

The outside of a bend in the river. The water will be deeper there. (R,S)

Shady places, particularly under trees and next to grassy banks, if the water is deep enough; especially if the sun is high. (S)

Near the bottom, where the current is slow and overhead predators cannot reach. (R,S)

Beneath overhead cover, such as logs and cut banks—especially brown trout, a species that is fond of overhead cover. In general, trout prefer cover that is parallel to the current. (S)

Drop-offs, depressions, and troughs in the bottom, often under fast water. The color of the water is one key to depth; the darker the water, the deeper it is. Shoals are indicated by lighter colored water. (R,S)

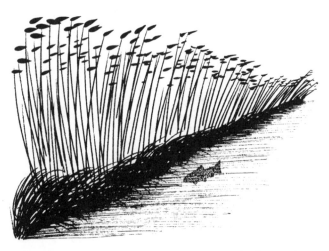

Figure 2-3. *Steep grassy banks and shade give some safety from predators and make fish feed more confidently.*

Flow

Figure 2-4. *Current moves slowly near the bottom, creating a resting place.*

Figure 2-5. *Overhead cover offers safety from some predators.*

Figure 2-6. *Drop-offs and depressions provide relief from current.*

Resting Places in Rivers   13

Figure 2-7. *Boulder fields offer protection.*

Down in weed beds, under floating weeds, or among reeds. (**S**)

Frothy, aerated water, especially late in the summer when the water is warm and the oxygen content is low. (**S,O**)

Down among boulders, if they are big enough to have hiding places in the crevices and holes. (**S,R**)

Near springs, if the general river temperature is extra cold or extra warm. Most springs are cold, but some waters have warm springs from geothermal activity. These can have a big impact on the fishing if the weather is cold. (**O; sometimes W**)

Note: Springs are hard to find. Sometimes they give away their presence by bubbles in the water, the presence of algae, or you may notice a sudden change in temperature. Local knowledge or maps can be a big help in locating springs.

Figure 2-8. *Springs offer cool, oxygenated water.*

Resting Places in Lakes

The criteria for good resting places in a lake are somewhat different from those in a river because there is rarely a need for relief from current. However, the need for oxygenated water (generally, cooler water) during hot weather may be greater than in rivers and sometimes this becomes the primary factor in determining resting places in lakes.

Resting places in lakes are described below with an indication of which criteria are met:

Safety from predators (S)

Oxygen in hot weather (O)

Warmth in cold weather (W)

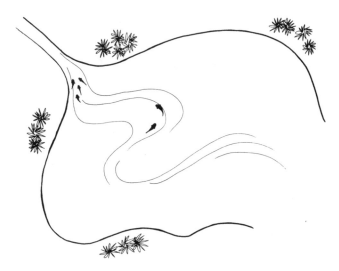

Figure 2-9. *The original streambed in a reservoir gives depth, concentrates food, and—at certain seasons—concentrates cooler, oxygenated water.*

Channels caused by inlet and outlet streams, or former streambeds in reservoirs. (**O**)

Note: many resorts on lakes will have a map showing the location of channels and, sometimes, springs. A good time to check out the location of channels is during the low water of late summer; map them out for later reference.

Deep water. The color of the water is the key to depth: lighter colored water is shallower. Trout may also be in deep water near cliffs. (**S**)

Shady places, particularly under trees or other vegetation if the water is deep enough. (**S**)

Among down or standing timber. (**S**)

Figure 2-10. *Weed beds, downed timber, standing timber—safe havens in lakes.*

Within weed beds, under floating weeds, or among reeds. **(S)**

Beneath overhead cover, such as floating logs—especially brown trout. **(S)**

Near springs. See notes on springs in the rivers section. **(O; sometimes W)**

Among large underwater boulders. **(S)**

Inlet streams. Inlet streams are always important in lakes, but there are two times when they are especially so: late in summer when the inlet water is cooler than the lake **(O)**; and during spawning season (generally, fall for brook and brown trout, spring for cutthroat and rainbow trout).

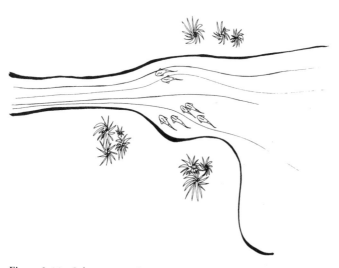

Figure 2-11. *Inlet areas can be a source of cool water during summer heat.*

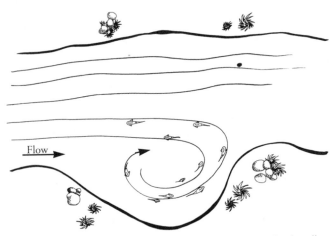

Flow →

Figure 2-12. *Back eddies are excellent food collectors, especially of smaller insects.*

Food Concentrations in Rivers

Trout food in rivers is concentrated in two areas: where it is produced, and where it is collected.

In general, trout in rivers prefer their food in places where the current collects it for them, such as in backeddies and current seams. Many food producing areas, such as shallow riffles, offer little protection for trout.

There are exceptions to the above. Some rivers have long riffles of sufficient depth to put trout at ease. Other rivers have long, smooth runs that generate large mayfly hatches, but there is nothing that concentrates the current and gathers the food. In these cases trout will take their food where it is produced.

The food concentrations shown below are separated into producing areas and collecting areas.

Finding the Trout

Food Producing Areas in Rivers

Riffles. Often these are food factories for aquatic insects, but unless there is a hatch in progress or many nymphs are being dislodged, fish will not be in shallow riffles.

Weed beds, more food factories.

Long runs with rocky bottoms.

Silty areas, which often support populations of midge larvae and burrowing mayfly nymphs.

Figure 2-13. *Trout often wait under trees for insects like caddisflies and stoneflies to be blown onto the water.*

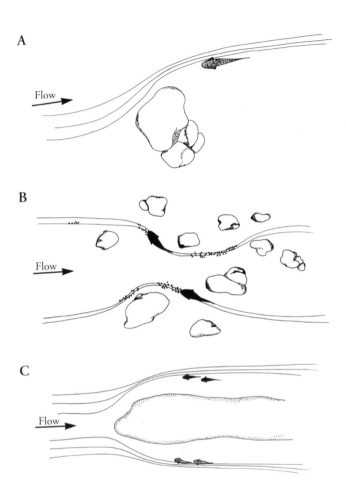

Figure 2-14. *Current seams.*
A—*Rock pushes current into narrow seam.*
B—*Foam line in boulder field shows where current and food concentrate.*
C—*Island creates current seam on both sides.*

Finding the Trout

Food Collecting Areas in Rivers

Back eddies. Back eddies are areas where the shoreline causes the current to go in large circles. Insects drifting downstream get trapped in them, and trout wait in the backeddy for food to come to them on an aquatic "lazy susan."

Downwind from trees and other streamside vegetation. Insects— both adult aquatics and terrestrials—are blown out of them onto the water.

Current seams created by obstructions like rocks or islands. Foam lines can be a key to mini-currents, such as those going through a boulder field: the same current that concentrated the foam concentrates the fish's food. Put your fly right in the foam line.

Current tongues. These are usually shaped like a letter "V" with the point downstream. Current—and therefore drifting food—is concentrated within the V. Trout often prefer the edges of the current tongue.

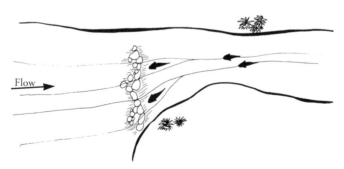

Figure 2-15. *Current tongues. In this example, Western March Browns (genus* Rhithrogena) *hatch in the rocky riffle, and trout wait downstream in the current tongues for drying duns.*

Food Concentrations in Lakes

Like rivers, lakes have areas that produce food and places that collect it. However, since there are fewer food collecting forces in lakes, trout there are more likely feed in the food-producing areas.

The food concentrations shown below are separated into producing and collecting areas.

Food Producing Areas in Lakes

In weed beds; a bug factory for lakes. Look for both underwater weeds and those that extend above the surface.

On and among down or standing timber; prime habitat for leeches and the nymphs of dragonflies and damselflies.

Silty areas, which often support populations of midge larvae and burrowing mayfly nymphs.

Shores with good exposure to the sun, especially in early season; usually this means southern and western shores, depending on where surrounding hills are and how tall they are.

Shallow areas where small fish will congregate — and big fish will come in and eat them — or where the sun will warm the water enough for insect activity.

Note: trout seldom feed in water over 15 feet deep; there just isn't much food down there.

Areas protected from wave action, such as bays. The protection allows insects to live unmolested—except by fish.

Gentle slopes, which allow vegetation and other insect habitat to accumulate. Islands and reefs often provide this feature, as well as some shoreline areas.

Note: areas with sandy bottoms which are exposed to heavy wind and wave action have little food. However, sometimes at dawn or

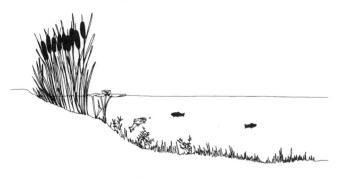

Figure 2-16. *Gentle slopes allow food to accumulate in lakes.*

Figure 2-17. *Drop-off near gentle slope in lake—food production with nearby safety.*

dusk minnows will gather here, and bigger fish will follow to feed on them. But in general, this is not productive water.

Food Collecting Areas in Lakes

Places with current (yes, even in lakes) such as the original river channel in reservoirs and near inlet and outlet streams.

Along windward shores. The food is blown in that direction.

Downwind from trees and other vegetation, if the water is deep enough to offer security to trout.

Where to Fish

Once you have identified resting places that are safe and easy, and places where food might be, look for places that offer both in one spot, such as a shady spot on the downstream and downwind side of an overhanging tree.

Your next best bet in rivers is a safe, easy place downstream from food concentration areas, such as in deeper, slower water just downstream from a riffle, or in slower water adjacent to a food-collecting current seam. Fish love transition zones such as these. They get a safe, easy place to rest and wait for food to be brought to them. Kind of like when your cousin Fred comes for Thanksgiving dinner.

It is a similar story in lakes. Look for food concentration zones adjacent to safe, resting water, such as a dropoff next to a gentle, shallow slope.

One good transition zone in rivers is where fast, shallow water suddenly changes to slow, deep water. This transition zone reveals itself as "restless" water—water with lots of bouncy riffles that aren't going anywhere.

Rivers are conveyor belts bringing food to the trout. The trout stay mostly in one place and wait for food to come to them. Lakes are different. Trout cruise about looking for food which may be mostly stationary, such as a midge pupa hanging in the surface film, or may be moving, such as a leech or rising caddis pupa. Often in lakes you need to fish different areas until you find the spots where the fish are concentrated.

When food is scarce, such as in winter, fish in rivers will tend to rest in quiet water conserving their energy.

Finding the BIG Fish

The largest, most aggressive fish will take the best places. "Best places" means places that offer the best combination of safety and easy food. For example, the head of a foam line in a river gives a

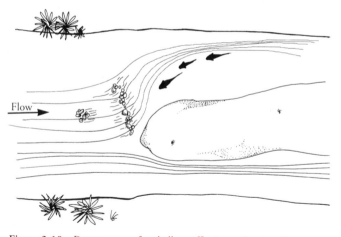

Figure 2-18. *Deeper water after shallow riffle. Insects live in riffle, get washed into current. Trout wait next to current seam between fast water and slow.*

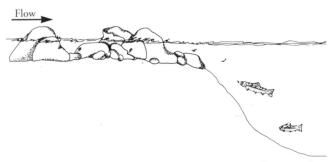

Figure 2-19. *Deep water following a riffle. Trout wait in deep water for food to be washed to them.*

big trout first pick of whatever comes downstream. Similarly, if a lake has a gently sloping area with a drop-off at the end, the big trout will be at the edges of the slope. That way they can forage for food but have quick access to the safety of the drop-off.

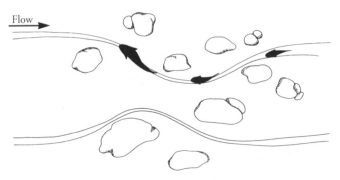

Figure 2-20. *Largest, most aggressive fish will be in best the places—first pick of food, closest to safety. Here, the largest trout is at the head of the foam line in a boulder field.*

In general, bigger fish are more aggressive than smaller fish. Also, browns and rainbows are more aggressive than brookies and cut-throat, and will take the best spots if the water has a mix of species.

It is important to keep these things in mind when planning your approach to the water. Otherwise you might spook a large trout by casting your line directly over it, or by hooking a small fish and dragging it past the larger fish.

Clues to Spotting Fish

Rise forms. You can sometimes tell which direction a fish is going by looking for a "V" in the rise form; if you see it, it points to where he went next.

Moving shadows on the bottom; in this case you must note where the sun is and do some mental geometry to locate the real fish.

Tails or fins of feeding fish sticking out of the water.

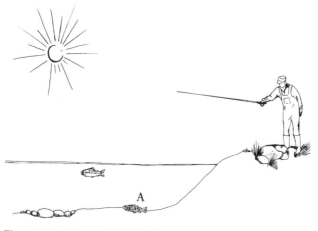

Figure 2-21. *You see the fish's shadow (A), but where is the fish?*

Gray shadows in the water.

A flash. Often this indicates a fish feeding on nymphs.

A puff of silt on the bottom; usually this is caused by a fish that just saw you and is trying to get away. Remember the place and come back to it later.

Movement that goes in a different direction, or at a different speed, than the current.

In moving water fish will keep their heads into the current, and the current where the fish is may be different than the current at the surface. This applies to lakes, also, where there is more current than most people realize. In lakes, fish very near the surface usually have their heads into the waves, which will be coming from the direction of the prevailing wind, while fish that are slightly deeper will be pointed in the opposite direction.

When you are moving, such as walking along the bank or drifting in a boat, it is hard to spot the subtle signs of fish feeding on emergers or the underwater flashes from nymphing trout. Stand in one place and concentrate your vision on the most likely places for fish to be.

Fish are rarely where you think you see them. In rivers they often rise from the bottom and follow a surface insect for several feet before taking it. This means you may have to cast upstream from where you saw the rise. In addition, there is refraction, the "bent" pencil in the water glass trick. Refraction makes submerged fish appear to be where they are not, and you must compensate: fish are deeper and closer to you than they appear.

Aids to Spotting Fish

To spot fish, use polarizing glasses to cut the glare from the water. Wear a hat with a long enough brim to block light from above, and cup your hands over the sides of your glasses to cut out the light from the sides.

When spotting fish, height is a big advantage. This is why osprey and eagles spot fish from the air, instead of standing on the bank scratching their heads like you and me.

Many anglers never get a chance to spot fish because their clothing or approach alerts the fish to their presence. The trout are gone before the angler even starts to look for them. See pages 173-177 for advice on approaching fish.

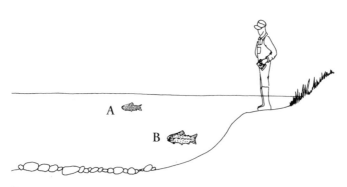

Figure 2-22. *Refraction makes fish appear shallower, farther out, and smaller. A—Fish appears here. B—Fish is really here.*

THREE

Choosing a Fly and Presentation

The ethics of pursuing trout with a fly rod evolved in a genteel English society that valued fair play and sportsmanship. Trout, on the other hand, pursue their own quarry—aquatic food—with no sporting instincts whatsoever. If trout could use dynamite to get mayflies they would do it.

Trout are not smart, as humans measure intelligence, but they understand one fact very well: they have to gain more energy from their food than they expend to capture it ... or they die. Eating an insect when it is helpless, with no defenses or means of escape, is not the depth of moral depravity to a trout; it is the pinnacle of good sense and the path of survival. Trout want "easy pickings."

Points of Vulnerability

The flyfisher should understand this concept of "easy pickings," or "points of vulnerability" to use a less vulgar phrase. Every insect species has its own points of high vulnerability based on its habitat and life cycle, and these points are generally predictable. Trout are capable of eating anything at anytime, but they *focus their feeding* at their food's points of highest vulnerability. Therefore, flyfishers should focus their efforts at these same points.

The Three Important Ingredients
in a Point of Vulnerability are:

The appearance of the insect, which the flyfisher matches with the appropriate choice of fly style and fly pattern.

The depth at which the point of vulnerability occurs. The flyfisher must present his fly at this depth.

The action of the insect at its point of vulnerability, which the fly-fisher must match with his presentation.

These are the *what, where,* and *how* of successful fly choice and presentation. If you don't match all three you will not be giving the trout what they are looking for.

Hard Times in a Bug's Life

Trout focus their feeding on distinct points of vulnerability—abbreviated as POV—in the life cycle of their prey. The POV concept includes the insect's appearance, depth, and behavior. These are imitated with the correct choice of fly pattern, presentation depth, and presentation tactic. It is not necessary to imitate all behavior of aquatic insects—just the most vulnerable behavior.

There are other POVs than the ones discussed here, some of which may be specific to a species and a particular body of water. The POVs in this handbook are the most common ones the fly-fisher will encounter, and the ones for which commercially tied flies are generally available. The creative angler will look for POVs that are not covered here and design flies and tactics to exploit them.

These POVs are dictated by the life cycle and habitat of the aquatic insects, and fall into three general areas: pre-adult, emergence, and adult, as detailed below.

Pre-Adult

Swimming. Some species of nymphs swim about searching for food or moving from one weedy area to another. A trout may intercept (and eat) it. Not all species swim, but those that do generally swim in the easiest current. In rivers, this means they will be near the bottom in faster water, or at almost any depth in slack water. In lakes, they could be at any depth, but they tend to be near aquatic vegetation and downed timber.

Figure 3-1. *Swimming POV — Damselfly nymph swimming near weedbed.*

Drifting. Nymphs drift for different reasons:

Behavioral drift. Every day, primarily near sunrise and sunset, a very small percentage of nymphs disperse by drifting a short distance in the current. However, since there are so many insects "a small percentage" can be enough to get the trout's attention. The genus *Baetis* is probably the best example of this behavior.

Figure 3-2. *Drifting POV — Stonefly nymph dislodged from rocky riffle.*

Accidental drift. A nymph or larva crawling on the bottom of a river may lose its grip on a rock and be swept along in the current.

Emergence

Migrating. Some nymphs and pupae emerge on vegetation and rocks. They crawl along the bottom to these when it is time to emerge, and often lose their grip and drift in the current … into the mouth of a waiting trout. Some species swim in great hoards to vegetation. Others migrate from faster water to slower water as they approach maturity. In each case, the insect exposes itself to hungry trout.

Rising. As a nymph or pupa (or sometimes a fully formed adult) leaves the bottom and rises to the surface, it is vulnerable to trout.

Figure 3-3 *Migrating POV — Stonefly nymphs crawling on the bottom to shore may be dislodged into the current.*

Figure 3-4 *— Damselfly and Gray Drake migrate to vegetation to emerge.*

Hard Times in a Bug's Life

Under the film. At the surface of the water, water molecules cling together. This is called "surface tension," and the air-water boundary is called the "meniscus," or simply "the film." To a large animal like a human the film is almost imperceptible, but to an insect the film is a springy, trampoline-like barrier that can be broken through only if they work at it hard enough. The nymph or pupa rises until it reaches the underside of the film. There, it must break through the film before it can fully emerge. This creates a hesitation in the rise … and makes them vulnerable. The smaller the insect, the bigger barrier the surface film presents to it. Thus, smaller insects are more likely to be taken as emergers just under the surface. Bigger, stronger species find the surface film to be less of a problem.

Hatching. Nymphs and pupae that emerge in open water must crawl out of their shucks before flying off. During this brief period they are helpless. Trout recognize this POV and will take hatching insects if they encounter them. During a hatch, trout usually hold in a feeding lane, or cruise a feeding zone, and take what comes to them. This means that they rarely selectively feed on the *hatching*

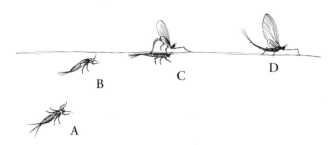

Figure 3-5. *Emergence POVs for many mayfly species.*
      A—Rising   *C—Hatching*
      B—Under film   *D—Drying dun*
Not all mayfly species exhibit these POVs.

POV, but they prefer it if they encounter it. Therefore the flyfisher who is trying to fish a "blizzard" hatch of midges or small mayflies, where the fake fly is among thousands of naturals, would do well to tie on a fly matching this POV as a way to distinguish his fly from the multitude of natural insects. Many fly shops have begun to carry commercially-tied flies that match this POV. This is an important POV for smaller insects like midges and most mayflies. It is less important for very large mayflies, caddisflies, and any insect that does not emerge in open water.

Drying dun. The winged insect that has emerged is rests *on the film*, which now works to its advantage as a support, and must dry its wings before it can take off. It is helpless … and trout know it. Larger mayflies take longer to dry their wings, and thus are more likely to be taken as duns than as emergers. For instance, the Western Green Drake (*Drunella grandis*) drifts for a long time and

Figure 3-6. *Emergence POVs for Quill Gordon (*Epeorus pleuralis*) and some other mayflies. Skin is shed underwater and dun rises to surface. POVs are rising, under the film, and drying dun. Use a downwing emerger for the first two POVs rather than a nymph. Hatching POV does not apply.*

is a sitting duck for the trout. On the other hand, many caddis-flies emerge on rocks and vegetation, and those that emerge in open water need no wing drying time. Midges emerge in open water, but like caddis they need no drying time. Stoneflies, dam-selflies, and dragonflies emerge on vegetation. Mayflies are therefore the only type of insect that have this point of vulnera-bility, but even some mayflies emerge out of the water and are not vulnerable at this stage.

Adult

Accident. Adult insects, especially caddis and stoneflies, often get blown off trees, grass, and other vegetation and land in the water. There they are temporarily stuck. During the caddis and stonefly seasons, trout often wait near the surface downstream from over-hanging vegetation, and nail anything that falls in the water and looks edible.

Ovipositing. Female insects must somehow get their eggs into the water as their last act of life. The act of egg-laying is called "ovipositing." Some of the ways they do this are: dipping to the surface, sprawling on the surface, swimming to the bottom, crawl-ing to the bottom, dropping eggs from above, and laying eggs on overhanging branches so that hatching larva will drop into the water later. Dippers may be imitated by "dapping" (see page 106), sprawlers with conventional dry fly presentations, and swimmers and crawlers (after they try to come back up) with wet fly and nymph techniques. There isn't much you can do to imitate drop-pers or branch layers unless they fall into the water.

Adult mayflies die shortly after egg laying, and their bodies often fall into the water with wings splayed out and lying in the film. These spent mayflies are known as "spinners" and trout will sometimes feed selectively on them. Floating spinner ties, with horizontal wings, are available to imitate them.

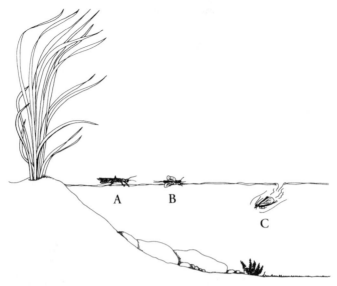

Figure 3-7. *Adult POVs.*
A—Stonefly blown from tree (accident).
B—Spent mayfly spinner (oviposit).
C—Female caddis swims under water to lay eggs (oviposit).

Points of Vulnerability Charts

The POV charts which follow on pages 44-79 describe common species of mayflies, stoneflies, midges and craneflies, damselflies, dragonflies, and caddisflies. For each POV there is a corresponding fly type, depth of presentation, and presentation tactic. See the next two pages for an explanation of the components of the charts.

There are several methods for determining which chart or charts to use. Selection might be based upon:

Finding out in advance which insects will be available at your destination. Published hatch charts, other experienced flyfishers, and fly shops are all good sources of this information.

Previous experience on this water at this time of year.

Some intelligent guessing.

Asking people who seem to know what they are doing. See Rule 1 in Chapter 1 first, though.

Identifying the mature aquatic insects in the water when you get there. This process is covered in depth in Chapter 5.

Explanation of Charts

1. *Title.* The general type of the insects covered on the chart, such as "Mayfly Swimmer" is in the title. Sometimes more than one chart is needed to cover all the species of one type. For instance, three charts are needed for mayfly swimmers in order to cover differences in emergence and habitat.

2. *Habitat.* The aquatic habitat of the nymph or larva is listed in general terms. For rivers, the habitats may be riffles, runs, pools, or the margins of the river. In lakes they are: shallow, weedy areas; silty bottoms; or pebbly, rocky shallows.

3. *Emergence.* The manner in which the adult typically emerges from the nymph or pupa.

4. *Family.* The scientific family name for the group of insects. See pages 90-91 for scientific naming conventions.

5. *Genus and Species.* When combined with the family name (see above) this identifies an insect within its order. See pages 90-91.

Not all genera and species are shown on the charts; only the ones the angler is most likely to encounter have been listed. The genus and species reflect current scientific literature, so some species have different names than those in long use by flyfishers; differences are noted on the charts.

6. *Common Name.* There may be more than one common name for an insect species, and often the same name is used for several different species. That's why there are scientific names—to avoid confusion. There is a cross reference of common names to scientific names following the charts on pages 82-89. Common names can be very confusing because of regional variations and the fact that they are often used incorrectly. Be aware that some words are used interchangeably, like *small, little,* and *tiny;* also, *big, large, great;* also, *dun, quill.* In addition, words like *Western* or *Eastern* that appear here and in other fly fishing literature are not usually used by people in the West or the East when referring to their bugs.

7. *Size.* Sizes do not include tails and antennae, and are shown in millimeters. A cross reference of millimeters to some standard hook sizes is found on pages 80-81.

8. *Distribution.* The general range of the species. E= East (east of Appalachians), W=West (Rockies to Pacific), M=Midwest.

9. *Emergence Season.* The season (winter, spring, summer, fall) in which the species emerges. Sometimes the emergence period starts a little before or extends a little past the primary season. These situations are indicated with a "←" or "→", respectively, in the primary season.

The emergence seasons shown on the charts are a general guide, so anglers may wish to record specific dates for their home waters. The author lives where he can traverse ecosystems ranging from coastal rain forests to temperate lowland valleys to alpine lakes to desert rivers in a three hour drive from his home. While he loves this ecological breadth, he freely admits it has blunted his enthusiasm for emergence charts that are not specific to a body of water.

10. *Points of Vulnerability.* There are 9 primary points of vulnerability:

Swimming
Drifting
Migrating
Rising
Under the film
Hatching
Drying dun
Accident
Ovipositing

These are discussed in detail on pages 32-39. Any given insect species typically exhibits only a limited number of these.

11. *Fly Type.* Types of fly patterns, including attractor patterns, are discussed on pages 91-97. For purposes of the charts, fly pattern types are:

Nymph/larva
Pupa
Emerger
Dry
Spinner
Submerged adult
Other

12. *Depth.* The proper depth for the point of vulnerability is generally:

On the surface film
In the surface film

Under the surface film (top 1 inch of water)

Near the surface (top 12 inches of water)

On the bottom (bottom 12 inches, or just above the weeds, which is as close as you can get)

Moving (either up or down, either near the surface or near the bottom)

Pages 98-101 discuss how to achieve the proper depth.

13. *Presentation Tactics.* Ten different presentations for rivers and six for lakes are discussed in detail on pages 101-107 and 108-111, respectively.

Note: The information in these charts is distilled from the author's personal experience, as well as a tall stack of fly fishing and entomology texts. While plowing through these tomes in pursuit of those few nuggets of information that a flyfisher for trout needs to know when on the water, the author encountered scientific fact, brilliant insight, wisdom, opinion, theory, error, amusing but unhelpful anecdotes, authors contradicting other authors, authors contradicting themselves, lots of BS, and not a few amazing gaps in our practical knowledge of aquatic insect behavior.

The author has tried to make the charts as useful and accurate as possible, but users of them should be aware that they are not gospel. There is no gospel in the world of aquatic insects. No doubt there are hatches of vast local importance that are not mentioned, common names that are omitted, emergence seasons that don't agree with local conditions, species sizes that are different than those listed here, and points of vulnerability the author has never dreamed of. And, waters where you don't need any charts because no matter what aquatic foods live there, all the trout rise with confidence to a #16 Adams.

1

Mayfly Crawlers —Olives and Green Drakes

Attenella, Danella, Drunella

Genus	Species	Common Name
Family: Ephemerellidae		
Attenella	*attenuatta*	Small Blue Winged Olive
A.	*margarita*	Little Blue Winged Olive
Danella	*simplex*	Small Blue Winged Olive
Drunella	*coloradensis*	Small Western Green Drake
D.	*cornuta*	Large Blue Winged Olive
D.	*cornutella*	Small Blue Winged Olive
D.	*doddsi*	Western Green Drake
D.	*flavilinea*	Small Western Green Drake
D.	*grandis*	Western Green Drake
D.	*lata*	Small Blue Winged Olive
D.	*longicornis*	Large Blue Winged Olive
D.	*spinifera*	Small Western Green Drake
D.	*walkeri*	Large Blue Winged Olive

POV	Fly Type	Depth
Drifting	Nymph	On the bottom
Rising	Nymph	Moving
Under the film	Nymph	Under the film
Hatching	Emerger	In the film
Drying dun	Dry	On the film
Ovipositing	Spinner	In the film

Note: Under the film *and* Hatching *are often the most important POVs for small species.*

Habitat: These mayflies live in rivers—riffles, runs, pools, margins.

Emergence: Nymph rises to surface in open water and dun emerges.

Size (mm)	Range	Winter	Spring	Summer	Fall
6-8	E M			←X	
6-7	E W			X	
7	E M			X	
11-12	W			X	
9-10	E M		X→		
6	E M			X	
14-16	W			←X	
8-10	W			X	
12-15	W			←X	
6-8	E M			X	
10	E			←X	
10-11	W			X	
9-10	E M			X	

Tactics

Deep nymph; especially hour or two before expected hatch
Rising nymph
Emerger, upstream or down
Dry, upstream or down
Dry, upstream or down
Dry, upstream or down

2

Mayfly Crawlers
Hendricksons, Pale Duns, Sulfurs

Ephemerella, Serratella

Genus	Species	Common Name
Family: Ephemerellidae		
Ephemerella	*dorothea*	Sulfur Dun, Pale Evening Dun
E.	*inermis*	Pale Morning Dun
E.	*infrequens*	Pale Morning Dun
E.	*invaria*	Pale Evening Dun, Sulfur Dun
E.	*rotunda*	Dark Hendrickson, Red Quill
E.	*subvaria*	Hendrickson, Red Quill
Serratella	*deficiens*	Little Dark Hendrickson
S.	*tibialis*	Small Western Dark Hendrickson

POV	Fly Type	Depth
Drifting	Nymph	On the bottom
Rising	Nymph	Moving
Under the film	Nymph	Under the film
Hatching	Emerger	In the film
Drying dun	Dry	On the film
Ovipositing	Spinner	In the film

Note: Under the film *and* Hatching *are often the most important POVs for small species.*

Habitat: These mayflies live in rivers--riffles, runs, pools, margins.

Emergence: Nymph rises to surface in open water and dun emerges.

Size (mm)	Range	Winter	Spring	Summer	Fall
7-8	E M		X→		
6-7	W			X→	
7-8	W			X→	
8-10	E M		X		
9-11	E M		X		
10-12	E M		X		
4-6	E M			X	
8	W			X	

Tactics

Deep nymph; especially hour or two before expected hatch
Rising nymph
Emerger, upstream or down
Dry, upstream or down
Dry, upstream or down
Dry, upstream or down

3

Mayfly Crawlers of Slow Water

Leptophlebia, Paraleptophlebia, Tricorythodes

Genus	Species	Common Name
Family: Leptophlebiidae		
Leptophlebia	*spp.*	Black Quill, Borcher's Dun
Paraleptophlebia	*adoptiva*	Slate Winged Mahogany Dun
P.	*bicornuta*	Large Slate Winged Mahogany Dun
P.	*debilis*	Dark Blue Quill, Slate Winged Mahogany Dun
P.	*helena*	Slate Winged Mahogany Dun
P.	*heteronea*	Slate Winged Mahogany Dun
P.	*mollis*	American Iron Blue Quill, Jenny Spinner
P.	*temporalis*	Blue Dun
Family: Tricorythodidae		
Tricorythodes	*spp.*	Trico, Tiny White Winged Black

POV	Fly Type	Depth
Drifting	Nymph	On the bottom
Migrating	Nymph	On the bottom
Rising	Nymph	Moving
Under the film	Nymph	Under the film
Hatching	Emerger	In the film
Drying dun	Dry	On the film
Ovipositing	Spinner	In the film

Note: Spinner stage *is the most important for Trico.*

Habitat: *Leptophlebia, Paraleptophlebia:* Rivers—sedimentary areas of riffles and runs. *Tricorythodes:* Rivers—pools, margins; Lakes—sand and silt areas among underwater vegetation.

Emergence: Nymph rises to surface in open water and dun emerges.

Size (mm)	Range	Winter	Spring	Summer	Fall
10-13	E M W		X→		
6-8	E M		X		
9-11	W			X→	
6-8	E M W			X	
9-11	W			X→	
7-8	W			←X	
6-8	E M			←X	
8-10	W		X	X	
3-4	E M W			X	X

Tactics

Deep nymph
Deep nymph; nymphs migrate to slower water as they mature, making
    them more available to trout
Rising nymph
Emerger, upstream or down
Dry, upstream or down
Dry, upstream or down
Dry, upstream or down

4

Mayfly Swimmers of the Lakes

Callibaetis

Genus	Species	Common Name
Family: Baetidae		
Callibaetis	*coloradensis*	Speckle Winged Quill
C.	*ferrugineus*	Speckle Winged Quill
C.	*fluctuans*	Speckle Winged Quill
C.	*nigritus*	Dark Speckle Winged Quill

POV	Fly Type	Depth
Swimming	Nymph	Near the surface
Rising	Nymph	Moving
Under the film	Nymph	Under the film
Hatching	Emerger	In the film
Drying dun	Dry	On the film
Ovipositing	Spinner	In the film

Note: *It is very difficult to accurately identify* Callibaetis *to the species level.*

Choosing a Fly and Presentation

Habitat: These mayflies live in lakes among underwater vegetation.

Emergence: Nymph rises to surface in open water and dun emerges.

Size (mm)	Range	Winter	Spring	Summer	Fall
7-9	M W		X	X	X
7-9	E M		X	X	X
6-7	E M		X	X	X
8-10	W		X	X	X

Tactics

Count down and retrieve; move about 12" of line in 2 seconds
a. Lift and settle beginning about 2 hours before the expected hatch
    b. Rising nymph
a. Chuck and sit with an occasional twitch
    b. Slow retrieve
Chuck and sit
Chuck and sit
Chuck and sit

5

Mayfly Swimmers of the Rivers

Baetis, Diphetor, Pseudocloeon

Genus	Species	Common Name
Family: Baetidae		
Baetis	*vagans*	Little Iron Blue Quill
B.	*spp.*	Blue Winged Olive
Diphetor	*hageni*	Blue Winged Olive
Pseudocloeon	*anoka*	Tiny Blue Winged Olive
P.	*carolina*	Blue Winged Olive
P.	*edmundsi*	Tiny Western Olive
P.	*futile*	Tiny Western Olive

POV	Fly Type	Depth
Drifting	Nymph	Bottom
Rising	Nymph	Moving
Under the film	Nymph	Under the film
Hatching	Emerger	In the film
Drying dun	Dry	On the film
Ovipositing	Spinner	In the film

Notes: All species are often referred to as Blue Winged Olives and Blue Duns.
All Baetis *species are difficult to distinguish from each other, especially the western species.*
Diphetor hageni *was previously classified as* Baetis parvus *and* Baetis hageni.

Habitat: *Baetis , Diphetor,* and *Pseudocloeon* are found in river riffles and runs. *Baetis* can also be found in the quieter waters of river pools, and along the margins, and in lakes, among underwater vegetation.

Emergence: Nymph rises to surface in open water and dun emerges.

Size (mm)	Range	Winter	Spring	Summer	Fall
7-8	E M		X		
3-12	E M W	X	X	X	X
6-7	E M W		X		←X
4-5	M			←X	
4-5	E		X	X	
4-5	W		X		←X
3-4	W			X→	

Tactics

Deep nymph; especially at sunrise and sunset, or all day during
    emergence periods
Rising nymph (in slow water)
Emerger, upstream or down
Dry, upstream or down
Dry, upstream or down
Dry, upstream or down

6

Mayfly Swimmers that Emerge out of the Water

Ameletus, Isonychia, Siphlonurus

Genus	Species	Common Name
Family: Oligoneuriidae		
Isonychia	*bicolor*	Leadwing Coachman, Dun Variant
I.	*harperi*	Leadwing Coachman, Dun Variant
I.	*sadleri*	Leadwing Coachman, White Gloved Howdy
I.	*velma*	Leadwing Coachman, Dun Variant
Family: Siphlonuridae		
Ameletus	*spp.*	none
Siphlonurus	*alternatus*	Gray Drake
S.	*occidentalis*	Gray Drake, Black Drake
S.	*quebecensis*	Gray Drake

POV	Fly Type	Depth
Swimming	Nymph	a. Bottom
		b. Near the surface
		c. Near the surface
Migrating	Nymph	Near the surface
Ovipositing	Spinner	In the film

Note: These species are not available to trout at emergence.

Habitat: *Ameletus:* Rivers—riffles, runs, pools, margins; *Isonychia:* Rivers—riffles, runs; *Siphlonurus:* Rivers—pools, margins, Lakes—among underwater vegetation and on silty bottoms of weedy areas.

Emergence: As nymphs mature they migrate to slower water, then crawl up onto vegetation or other objects that are above water. Duns emerge there.

Size (mm)	Range	Winter	Spring	Summer	Fall
13-16	E M			←X	
12-14	E M				←X
13-16	E M			←X	
13-16	W			X	
9-14	E M W		X	X	X
13-16	E M W		X→		
14-18	M W			X	X
12-15	E M		X		

Tactics

Deep nymph
Wet fly swing
Slow retrieve
Retrieve from midriver to slower or shallower water; begin trying 2-3
    weeks before expected emergence
Dry, upstream or down

7

Mayfly Clingers that Usually Emerge on the Surface

Cinygmula, Rhithrogena, Stenonema

Genus	Species	Common Name
Family: Heptageniidae		
Cinygmula	*ramaleyi*	Small Western Gordon Quill
C.	*reticulata*	Pale Brown Dun
C.	*subequalis*	Small Gordon Quill
Rhithrogena	*hageni*	March Brown, Black Quill
R.	*morrisoni*	March Brown, Black Quill
R.	*undulata*	Red Quill
Stenonema	*fuscum*	Gray Fox, Ginger Quill
S.	*ithaca*	Gray Fox, Light Cahill
S.	*interpunctatum*	Cahill, Gray Fox
S.	*vicarium*	American March Brown, Dark Cahill

POV	Fly Type	Depth
Rising	Nymph	Moving
Under the film	Nymph	Under the film
Hatching	Emerger	In the film
Drying dun	Dry	On the film
Ovipositing	Spinner	In the film

Notes: Clinger nymphs like these are rarely available to trout until emergence, however migration to slower water shortly before emergence can make them vulnerable.

Genera on this chart generally emerge on the surface, but some will emerge underwater; try the tactics in Chart 8 for them.

Habitat: *Cinygmula:* Rivers—riffles, runs; *Rhithrogena:* Rivers—riffles, runs; *Stenonema* mayflies are found in both rivers (riffles, runs, pools, margins) and lakes (shallow, rocky shores).

Emergence: Nymphs rise to surface in open water and dun emerges. Genera on this chart often migrate to slower water prior to emergence.

Size (mm)	Range	Winter	Spring	Summer	Fall
6-8	W				X
8	W				X
8-9	E				←X
9-10	W		X→		
8-9	W	X→			
7-8	M W			X	
12-14	E M		X→		
10-12	E			←X	
12-14	E M			←X	
14-16	E M		X→		

Tactics

Rising nymph
Emerger, upstream or down
Dry, upstream or down
Dry, upstream or down
Dry, upstream or down

8

Mayfly Clingers that Usually Emerge Underwater

Heptagenia, Leucrocuta, Epeorus

Genus	Species	Common Name
Family: Heptageniidae		
Heptagenia	*elegantula*	Western Pink Quill, Pale Evening Dun
H.	*simplicoides*	Western Ginger Quill, Pale Evening Dun
Leucrocuta	*hebe*	Small Grey Winged Yellow Quill
Epeorus	*albertae*	Western Gordon Quill
E.	*deceptivus*	Little Blue Quill
E.	*longimanus*	Western Gordon Quill
E.	*pleuralis*	Quill Gordon
E.	*vitreus*	Gray Winged Yellow Quill, Sulfur Dun

POV	Fly Type	Depth
Rising	Emerger	Moving
Under the film	Emerger	Near the surface
Drying Dun	Dry	On the film
Ovipositing	Spinner	In the film

Notes: Clinger nymphs like these are rarely available until emergence.
Genera on this chart generally emerge under water but a few species sometimes emerge on the surface so the tactics in Chart 7 can be appropriate for them.
Luecrocuta *was formerly classified as* Heptagenia.

Habitat: *Epeorus* and *Heptagenia:* Rivers—riffles, runs; *Leucrocuta:* Rivers—riffles, runs, pools, margins.

Emergence: Dun usually emerges underwater and rises to surface in open water.

Size (mm)	Range	Winter	Spring	Summer	Fall
8-10	W			X	
9-10	W			X	
6-8	E M			X→	
9-11	W			X	
8-9	W			X	
10-11	W			X	
9-12	E		X→		
9-12	E M			←X	

Tactics

a. Rising nymph
　b. Wet fly swing
Emerger, upstream or down
Dry, upstream or down
Dry, upstream or down

9

Mayfly Burrowers

Ephoron, Ephemera, Hexagenia, Litobrancha, Potamanthus

Genus	Species	Common Name
Family: Polymitarcyidae		
Ephoron	*album*	White Drake
E.	*leukon*	White Drake
Family: Ephemeridae		
Ephemera	*guttulata*	Eastern Green Drake, Coffin Fly
E.	*simulans*	Brown Drake
E.	*varia*	Yellow Drake, Cream Variant
Hexagenia	*limbata*	Great Yellow May, Sandfly, Michigan Caddis, Fishfly, Great Lead Winged Drake
Litobrancha	*recurvata*	Dark Green Drake
Family: Potamanathidae		
Potamanthus	*distinctus*	Yellow Drake, Cream Variant

POV	Fly Type	Depth
Rising	Nymph	a. Near the bottom
		b. Moving
Hatching	Emerger	In the film
Drying dun	Dry	On the film
Ovipositing	Spinner	In the film

Notes: Nymphs *are not generally available to trout until emergence.*
Rising *is the most important POV.*
Litobrancha was *previously classified in* Hexagenia.

Habitat: *Ephoron* and *Hexagenia* mayflies prefer silty bottom areas of lakes and rivers. In rivers they are found primarily in pools and margins. *Potamanthus* and *Litobrancha* species prefer the same habitat but are found only in rivers. *Ephemera* mayflies prefer sand and gravel bottom areas of both rivers and lakes.

Emergence: Nymphs leave burrows on bottom and rise to surface in open water where dun emerges.

Size (mm)	Range	Winter	Spring	Summer	Fall
11-12	M W			X→	
13-14	E M			X	
18-30	E		X→		
11-14	E M W		X	X	
13-16	E M			X	
16-35	E M W			X	
16-38	E M		X→		
13-16	E M				X

Tactics

Lift and settle; raise the nymph several feet off the bottom, and let it
    drop back. Begin several hours before hatch is expected to start.
Rising nymph
Chuck and sit
Chuck and sit
Chuck and sit

10

Large Stoneflies

Genus	Species	Common Name
Family: Pteronarcyidae		
Pteronarcella	*badia*	Small Salmonfly
Pteronarcys	*californica*	Salmonfly, Giant Stonefly
P.	*dorsata*	Giant Black Stonefly
Family: Perlidae		
Acroneuria	*lycorias*	Great Brown Stonefly
A.	*pacifica*	(now classified as Hesperoperla pacifica)
Attaneuria	*ruralis*	Yellow Legged Stonefly
Calineuria	*californica*	Golden Stonefly
Hesperoperla	*pacifica*	Willowfly, Brown Stonefly, Brown Willowfly
Perlesta	*spp.*	Great Stonefly
Phasganophora	*capitata*	Great Stonefly

POV	Fly Type	Depth
Drifting	Nymph	Bottom
Migrating	Nymph	Bottom
Accident	Dry	On the film
Ovipositing	Dry	On the film

Notes: In rivers that have big populations of large stoneflies, trout will feed on the nymphs all year.
Large stoneflies are not available to trout at emergence.

Habitat: Large stoneflies live in rivers, and are found primarily riffles and runs, except during migration.

Emergence: As nymphs mature, they crawl along the bottom to shore, then up onto vegetation or other objects that are above water. Adults emerge there. During migration many nymphs are knocked loose into the current and are taken by trout.

Size (mm)	Range	Winter	Spring	Summer	Fall
25-40	W		X→		
25-50	W		X→		
35-55	E M W		X	X	
22-35	E M		X	X	
22-35	E M		X		
24-38	W			←X	
22-35	W		X		
25-38	E M			X	
25-38	E M		X		

Tactics

Deep nymph in fast, riffled water, or in the transition from fast water to
   slower water
Deep nymph in or near fast water
a. Dry, upstream or down; near vegetation when adults are present
   b. Skating
Dry, upstream or down

11

Small Stoneflies

Genus	Species	Common Name
Family: Capniidae		Early Black Stonefly, Winter Stonefly
Family: Chloroperlidae		
Alloperla	*spp.*	Little Green Stonefly
Sweltsa	*spp.*	Little Olive Stonefly
Family: Leuctridae		Needlefly
Family: Nemouridae		
Malenka	*spp.*	Little Western Stonefly, Little Brown Stonefly
Zapada	*spp.*	Little Sepia Stonefly, Little Brown Stonefly
Family: Perlodidae		
Isogenoides	*spp.*	Early Orange Stonefly
Isoperla	*bilineata*	Little Yellow Stonefly
I.	*mormona*	Western Yellow Stonefly
I.	*signata*	Light Stonefly, Light Brown Stonefly
Family: Taeniopterygidae		
Strophopteryx fasciata		Early Brown Stonefly, Little Red Stonefly

POV	Fly Type	Depth
Migrating	Nymph	Bottom
Accident	Dry	On the film
Ovipositing	Dry	On the film

Notes: Nymphs of most species are not generally available until they migrate. Small stoneflies are not available to trout at emergence.

Habitat: All live in rivers. Capniidae and Leuctridae, *Isoperla, Isogenoides, and Strophopteryx* prefer the faster waters of riffles and runs, except during migration. The others can be found in riffles, runs, pools and margins.

Emergence: As nymphs mature, they crawl along the bottom to shore, then up onto vegetation or other objects that are above water. Adults emerge there. During migration many nymphs are knocked loose into the current and are taken by trout.

Size (mm)	Range	Winter	Spring	Summer	Fall
6-10	E M W	X→			X
7-12	E M			X	
7-12	E M W			X	
7-13	E M W	X	X	X	X
7-12	W	X	X		
7-12	E M W	X	X		
13-22	E W		X→		
9-15	E M		X→		
7-16	W		X	X	
7-16	E M		X→		
10-15	E	X	X		

Tactics

Deep nymph beginning one or two weeks before emergence
Dry, upstream or down
Dry, upstream or down

12

Midges and Craneflies

Genus	Species	Common Name
Family: Chironomidae		Chironomid, Midge
Family: Tipulidae		Crane Fly
Family: Blephariceridae		Netwinged Midge
Family: Dixidae		Dixid Midge

POV	Fly Type	Depth
Rising	Pupa	Moving
Under the film	Pupa	Under the film
Hatching	Emerger	In the film
Accident	Dry	On the film

Notes: Entomologists' division of these families into over 1,000 species is not helpful to flyfishers.

Species in the families Blephariceridae and Dixidae are often mistaken for Crane Flies, and can be more important than true Crane Flies in running water.

Midge hatches are very common—even dominant—at dusk on lakes. They can also be common in early morning.

The primary POV is under the film for midges.

Midge sizes shown here are typical. There are both smaller and larger species.

Habitat: Chironomidae, Tipulidae — all water habitats; Dixidae — rivers (riffles, runs, pools, margins); Blephariceridae — rivers (riffles, runs).

Emergence: Pupa rises to surface of open water where adult emerges.

Size (mm)	Range	Winter	Spring	Summer	Fall
2-12	E M W	X	X	X	X
10-25	E M W		X	X	X
4-12	E W	X	X	X	X
3-7	E M W	X	X	X	X

Tactics

Rising nymph; not generally useful for rivers, but works well in lakes
a. Midge pupa (lakes)
  b. Emerger, upstream or down (rivers) in slow water and back
  eddies
  c. Slow retrieve (lakes)
Chuck and sit (lakes)
Chuck and sit (lakes)

13

Damselflies

Genus	Species	Common Name
Family: Calopterygidae		
Calopteryx	*spp.*	Bandwings, Ruby Spots
Family: Coenagrionidae		
Argia	*spp.*	Dancers
Enallagma	*spp.*	Bluets
Ischnura	*spp.*	Forktails
Family: Lestidae		
Lestes	*spp.*	Marsh Spreadwings

POV	Fly Type	Depth
Swimming	Nymph	All depths, but especially near the surface
Migrating	Nymph	All depths, but especially near the surface
Ovipositing	Dry	On the film

Note: Damselflies are not available to trout at emergence.

Habitat: *Calopteryx* and *Argia* are both found in rivers—riffles, runs, pools, margins. *Argia* is also found in silty and shallow rocky areas of lakes. *Enallagma, Ischnura,* and *Lestes* are found among underwater vegetation and in the pools and margins of rivers and in lakes.

Emergence: Nymphs migrate by swimming to above-water objects like rocks and vegetation. They climb out of the water and the adult emerges.

Size (mm)	Range	Winter	Spring	Summer	Fall
25-55	E M W		X	X	
15-40	E M W			←X	
20-40	E M W		X	X	
15-35	E M W		X	X	
20-45	E M W		X	X	

Tactics

Count down and retrieve. Move about 18 inches of line in about 3 seconds, then pause 3 seconds. Retrieve near areas of weeds and downed timber.

Same as *swimming* POV, but retrieve towards above-surface objects like vegetation or rocks.

Chuck and sit

14

Dragonflies

Genus	Species	Common Name
Family: Aeshnidae		
Aeshna	*spp.*	Blue Darners
Anax	*spp.*	Green Darners

POV	Fly Type	Depth
Swimming	Nymph	All depths, but especially near the surface
Migrating	Nymph	All depths, but especially near the surface

Notes: Dragonflies are not available to trout at emergence.
Ovipositers are not generally available to trout.

Habitat: Dragonflies live in lakes among underwater vegetation.

Emergence: Nymphs migrate by swimming to above-water objects like rocks and vegetation. They climb out of the water and the adult emerges.

Size (mm)	Range	Winter	Spring	Summer	Fall
35-80	E M W		X	X	
40-85	E M W		X	X	

Tactics

Count down and retrieve. Move 2-6 inches of line in one second then pause briefly and repeat. Retrieve near areas of weeds and downed timber.

Same as *swimming* POV, but retrieve towards above-surface objects like vegetation or rocks.

15

Saddle-Case Caddis and Micro Caddis

Genus	Species	Common Name
Family: Glossosomatidae		
Glossosoma	*spp.*	Little Tan Short Horn Sedge, Saddle-Case Caddis
Family: Hydroptilidae		Micro Caddis

POV	Fly Type	Depth
Rising	Pupa	Bottom
Under the film	Pupa	Under the film
Accident	Dry	On the film
Ovipositing	a. Submerged adult	Near the surface
	b. Dry	On the film

Notes: Larvae are not generally available to trout, however a caseless Glossosoma *larval imitation fished with deep nymph tactics can sometimes be productive at dawn and dusk.*

Habitat: Saddle-Case Caddis live in rivers (riffles, runs); Micro Caddis are in both rivers (riffles, runs, pools, margins) and lakes (rocky shores and among underwater vegetation)

Emergence: Pupae of some species swim to surface of water where adults immediately emerge and fly away. Pupae of other species crawl to shore and emerge on vegetation or other objects that are above water.

Size (mm)	Range	Winter	Spring	Summer	Fall
5-10	E M W		←X	X→	
3-5	E M W			X	

Tactics

Deep nymph
a. Emerger, upstream or down
  b. Wet fly swing
a. Dry, upstream or down
  b. Skating
Wet fly swing
a. Dry, upstream or down
  b. Dapping

16

Free-Living and Net-Spinning Caddis

Genus	Species	Common Name
Family: Rhyacophilidae *(free living)*		
Rhyacophila	spp.	Green Rock Worm, Green Sedge
Family: Hydropsychidae *(net-spinning)*		
Arctopsyche	spp.	Great Gray Spotted Sedge
Cheumatopsyche	spp.	Little Sister Sedge
Hydropsyche	spp.	Spotted Sedge
Family: Philopotamidae *(net-spinning)*		
Chimarra	spp.	Little Black Sedge
Wormaldia	spp.	Little Autumn Stream Sedge
Family: Polycentropodidae *(net-spinning)*		
Polycentropus	spp.	Brown Checkered Summer Sedge
Family: Psychomyiidae *(net-spinning)*		
Psychomyia	spp.	Dinky Purple-Breasted Sedge

POV	Fly Type	Depth
Drifting	Larva	Bottom
Rising	Pupa	Bottom
Under the film	Pupa	Under the film
Accident	Dry	On the film
Ovipositing	a. Submerged adult	Near the surface
	b. Dry	On the film

Choosing a Fly and Presentation

Habitat: Rivers—riffles, runs; some *Polycentropus* species live among underwater vegetation in lakes.

Emergence: Pupae of some species swim to surface, emerge, and fly away. Pupae of other species crawl to shore and emerge on vegetation or other objects above water.

Size (mm)	Range	Winter	Spring	Summer	Fall
7-15	E M W		X	X→	
15-25	E W			X	
8-12	E M W		X	X	
10-15	E M W		X	X	X
6-10	E M		X→		
8-12	E M W		X		X
8-12	E M W			←X	
4-8	E M W		X	X	

Tactics

Deep nymph
Deep nymph
a. Emerger, upstream or down
   b. Wet fly swing
a. Dry, upstream or down
   b. Skating
Wet fly swing
a. Dry, upstream or down
   b. Dapping

17

River-Dwelling (Mostly) Tube-Case Caddis

Genus	Species	Common Name
Family: Brachycentridae		
Brachycentrus	*spp.*	Grannom
Family: Lepidostomatidae		
Lepidostoma	*spp.*	Little Plain Brown Sedge
Family: Leptoceridae		
Nectopsyche	*spp.*	White Miller
Oecetis	*spp.*	Long Horn Sedge
Family: Limnephilidae		
Dicosmoecus	*spp.*	Giant Orange Sedge, October Caddis
Hydatophylax	*spp.*	Giant Cream Sedge
Neophylax	*spp.*	Autumn Mottled Sedge
Pycnopsyche	*spp.*	Great Brown Autumn Sedge
Family: Odontoceridae:		
Psilotreta	*spp.*	Dark Blue Sedge

POV	Fly Type	Depth
Drifting	Larva	Bottom
Rising	Pupa	Bottom
Under the film	Pupa	Under the film
Accident	Dry	On the film
Ovipositing	a. Submerged adult	Near the surface
	b. Dry	On the film

Habitat: All genera on this chart are found in rivers.
Dicosmoecus, Neophylax—riffles, runs
Hydatophylax—pools, margins
Brachycentrus—riffles, runs among underwater vegetation and downed timber
Lepidostoma—riffles, runs, pools, margins

The following genera have some species which also occur in lakes:
Oecetis, Pycnopsyche—riffles, runs, pools, margins
Psilotreta—riffles, runs, pools, margins; especially gravelly areas
Nectopsyche—riffles, runs, pools, margins among underwater vegetation

Emergence: Pupae of some species swim to surface emerge and fly away. Pupae of other species crawl to shore and emerge above water.

Size (mm)	Range	Winter	Spring	Summer	Fall
10-13	E M W		X	X	
8-10	E M W		X	X	
10-17	E M W			←X	
9-12	E M W		X	X	
20-30	W				←X
25-34	E M W			X→	
10-15	E M W				←X
18-25	E M			X	X
10-15	E		X→		

Tactics

Deep nymph
Deep nymph
a. Emerger, upstream or down
    b. Wet fly swing
a. Dry, upstream or down
    b. Skating
Wet fly swing
a. Dry, upstream or down
    b. Dapping

18

Lake-Dwelling (Mostly) Tube-Case Caddis

Genus	Species	Common Name
Family: Limnephilidae		
Lenarchus	*spp.*	Dark Brown Stillwater Sedge
Limnephilus	*spp.*	Summer Flier Sedge
Family: Molannidae		
Molanna	*spp.*	Gray Checkered Sedge
Family: Phryganeidae		
Banksiola	*spp.*	Traveller Sedge

POV	Fly Type	Depth
Rising	Pupa	To surface
Under the film	Pupa	Under the film
Accident	Dry	On the film
Ovipositing	a. Dry	On the film
	b. Submerged adult	Moving

Note: Larval stage *is not generally important.*

Habitat: *Lenarchus* species are found in the shallow areas of lakes.
Limnephilus— in all areas, some species in rivers
Molanna— shallow rocky areas, some species in rivers
Banksiola— weedy areas of lakes, some species in rivers

Emergence: Pupae of some species swim to surface where adults immediately emerge and fly away. Pupae of other species crawl to shore and emerge on vegetation or other objects that are above water.

Size (mm)	Range	Winter	Spring	Summer	Fall
18-22	W			X	
13-20	E M W		X	X	X
10-16	E M W			←X	
15-25	E M W			X	

Tactics

Rising nymph
a. Chuck and sit
    b. Slow retrieve
Chuck and sit
Chuck and sit
Rising nymph

Shank Length mm	Hook Sizes for a Given Shank Length (Millimeters) — Tiemco Hooks				
	TMC Hook Type				
	100	3769	3761	5263	300
3					
3.5	26				
4	24	18			
4.5	22				
5	20				
5.5		16	18		
6	18				
6.5					
7	16	14	16	18	
7.5					
8	14	12	14	16	
9	12	10	12		
10		8	10	14	
11	10				
12		6		12	
13	8				
14			8	10	
15	6				14
16				8	
17					
18					12
19					
20	4			6	
21					10
24					8
25				4	
27					6
30				2	
31					
32					4
36					2

Choosing a Fly and Presentation

Shank Length mm	Hook Sizes for a Given Shank Length (Millimeters) — Mustad Hooks				
	Mustad Hook Type				
	94845	3906	3906B	9671	9672
3	28				
3.5	26	20			
4	24				
4.5	22	18			
5					
5.5	20	16	18		
6					
6.5	18	14			
7	16		16	18	
7.5	14	12			
8	12		14	16	
9		10			
10		8	12	14	16
11	10			12	14
12	8	6	10		
13				10	12
14		4	8		
15	6			8	10
16	4				
17			6		8
18		2		6	
19			4		
20	2				6
21				4	
24					
25					4
27			2		
30					
31					2
32					
36					

Common Name to Scientific Name Cross Reference

Common Name	Scientific Name	Chart
American March Brown	*Stenonema vicarium*	8
American Iron Blue Quill	*Paraleptophlebia mollis*	3
Autumn Mottled Sedge	*Neophylax spp.*	17
Bandwings	*Calopteryx spp.*	13
Black Drake	*Siphlonurus spp.*	6
Black Quill	*Leptophlebia spp.*	3
	Rhithrogena hageni	7
	R. morrisoni	7
Blue Darners	*Aeshna spp.*	13
Blue Dun	*Paraleptophlebia temporalis*	3
	Pseudocloeon spp.	5
Bluets	*Enallagma spp.*	13
Blue Winged Olive	*Attenella attenuatta*	1
	A. margarita	1
	Baetis spp.	5
	Danella simplex	1
	Diphetor hageni	5
	Drunella cornuta	1
	D. cornutella	1
	D. lata	1
	D. longicornis	1
	D. walkeri	1
	Pseudocloeon spp.	5
Borcher's Dun	*Leptophlebia spp.*	3
Brown Checkered Summer Sedge	*Polycentropus spp.*	16
Brown Drake	*Ephemera simulans*	9

Brown Stonefly	*Hesperoperla pacifica*	10
Brown Willowfly	*Hesperoperla pacifica*	10
Cahill	*Stenonema interpunctatum*	8
	S. ithaca	8
Chironomid	Chironomidae family	12
Coffin Fly	*Ephemera guttulata*	9
Cranefly	Tipulidae family	12
Cream Variant	*Ephemera varia*	9
	Potamanthus distinctus	9
Damselfly	*Argia spp.*	13
	Calopteryx spp.	13
	Enallagma spp.	13
	Ischnura spp.	13
	Lestes spp.	13
Dancers	*Argia spp.*	13
Dark Blue Sedge	*Psilotreta spp.*	17
Dark Blue Quill	*Paraleptophlebia debilis*	3
Dark Brown Spinner	*Paraleptophlebia spp.*	3
Dark Brown Stillwater Sedge	*Lenarchus spp.*	18
Dark Cahill	*Stenonema vicarium*	8
Dark Green Drake	*Litobrancha recurvata*	9
Dark Hendrickson	*Ephemerella rotunda*	2
Dark Speckle Winged Quill	*Callibaetis nigritus*	4
Dinky Purple-Breasted Sedge	*Psychomyia spp.*	15
Dixid Midge	Dixidae family	12
Dragonfly	*Aeshna spp.*	14
	Anax spp.	14
Dun Variant	*Isonychia spp.*	6
Early Black Stonefly	Capniidae family	11

Early Brown Stonefly	*Strophopteryx fasciata*	11
Early Orange Stonefly	*Isogenoides spp.*	11
Eastern Green Drake	*Ephemera guttulata*	9
Fishfly	*Hexagenia limbata*	9
Forktails	*Ischnura spp.*	13
Giant Black Stonefly	*Pteronarcys dorsata*	10
Giant Cream Sedge	*Hydatophylax spp.*	17
Giant Mayfly	*Hexagenia limbata*	9
Giant Orange Sedge	*Dicosmoecus spp.*	17
Giant Salmonfly	*Pteronarcys californica*	10
Giant Stonefly	*Pteronarcys californica*	10
Ginger Quill	*Stenonema fuscum*	8
	S. spp.	8
Golden Drake	*Potamanthus distinctus*	9
Golden Stonefly	*Calineuria californica*	10
Gordon Quill	*Epeorus pleuralis*	8
Grannom	*Brachycentrus spp.*	17
Gray Checkered Sedge	*Molanna spp.*	18
Gray Drake	*Siphlonurus spp.*	6
Gray Fox	*Stenonema fuscum*	8
	S. interpunctatum	8
	S. ithaca	8
Gray Winged Yellow Quill	*Epeorus vitreus*	8
Great Brown Autumn Sedge	*Pycnopsyche spp.*	17
Great Brown Stonefly	*Acroneuria lycorias*	10
Great Gray Spotted Sedge	*Arctopsyche spp.*	16
Great Leadwing Drake	*Hexagenia limbata*	9
Great Stonefly	*Perlesta spp.*	10

	Phasganophora capitata	10
Great Yellow Mayfly	*Hexagenia limbata*	9
Green Darners	*Anax spp.*	14
Green Drake	*Ephemera guttulata*	9
	Drunella colorandensis	1
	D. doddsi	1
	D. flavilinea	1
	D. grandis	1
	D. spinifera	1
Green Rock Worm	*Rhyacophila spp.*	16
Green Sedge	*Rhyacophila spp.*	16
Hendrickson	*Ephemerella subvaria*	2
Iron Blue Dun	*Paraleptophlebia adoptiva*	3
Jenny Spinner	*Paraleptophlebia mollis*	3
Large Blue Winged Olive	*Drunella cornuta*	1
	D. longicornis	1
	D. walkeri	1
Lrg. Slate Winged Mahogany Dun	*Paraleptophlebia bicornuta*	3
Leadwing Coachman	*Isonychia spp.*	6
Light Brown Stonefly	*Isoperla signata*	11
Light Cahill	*Stenonema ithaca*	8
Light Stonefly	*Isoperla signata*	11
Little Autumn Stream Sedge	*Wormaldia spp.*	16
Little Black Sedge	*Chimarra spp.*	16
Little Blue Quill	*Epeorus deceptivus*	8
Little Blue Winged Olive	*Attenella attenuatta*	1
	A. margarita	1
Little Brown Stonefly	*Malenka spp.*	11
	Zapada spp.	11

	H. simplicoides	7
	Ephemerella dorothea	2
	Epeorus vitreus	8
Pale Morning Dun	*Ephemerella inermis*	2
	Ephemerella infrequens	2
Quill Gordon	*Epeorus pleuralis*	8
Red Quill	*Ephemerella rotunda*	2
	E. subvaria	2
	Rhithrogena undulata	7
Ruby Spots	*Calopteryx spp.*	13
Salmonfly	*Pteronarcys californica*	10
Sandfly	*Hexagenia limbata*	9
Slate Cream Dun	*Epeorus albertae*	8
Slate Winged Mahogany Dun	*Paraleptophlebia spp.*	3
Slate Winged Olive	*Attenella attenuatta*	1
	Drunella flavilinea	1
	D. lata	1
Small Blue Winged Olive	*Danella simplex*	1
	Drunella cornutella	1
	D. lata	1
Small Gray Winged Yellow Quill	*Leucrocuta hebe*	7
Small Green Drake	*Drunella coloradensis*	1
	D. spinifera	1
Small Salmonfly	*Pteronarcella badia*	10
Small Western Gordon Quill	*Cinygmula ramaleyi*	3
Small Western Green Drake	*Drunella coloradensis*	1
	D. flavilinea	1
	D. spinifera	1
Speckle Winged Quill	*Callibaetis spp.*	4

Spotted Sedge	*Hydropsyche spp.*	16
Sulfur Dun	*Ephemerella dorothea*	2
	E. invaria	2
	Epeorus vitreus	8
Summer Flier Sedge	*Limnephilus spp.*	18
Tiny Blue Winged Olive	*Pseudocloeon anoka*	5
	P. edmundsi	5
Tiny Western Olive	*Pseudocloeon edmundsi*	5
	P. futile	5
Tiny White Winged Black	*Tricorythodes spp.*	3
Traveller Sedge	*Banksiola spp.*	18
Trico	*Tricorythodes spp.*	3
Western Gordon Quill	*Epeorus albertae*	8
	E. longimanus	8
Western Green Drake	*Drunella doddsi*	1
	D. grandis	1
Western Ginger Quill	*Heptagenia simplicoides*	7
Western March Brown	*Rhithrogena morrisoni*	7
	R. hageni	7
Western Pink Quill	*Heptagenia elegantula*	7
Western Yellow Stonefly	*Isoperla mormona*	11
Whirling Dun	*Leptophlebia spp.*	3
White Drake	*Ephoron album*	9
	E. leukon	9
White Winged Black	*Tricorythodes spp.*	3
White Winged Curse	*Tricorythodes spp.*	3
White Gloved Howdy	*Isonychia sadleri*	6
White Miller	*Nectopsyche spp.*	17

Scientific Classification of Insects

The red plague rid you for learning me your language.
The Tempest

Terminology

Biologists organize living creatures into groups. Insects are a class. The class is successively subdivided into order, family, genus, and species. The scientific format for identifying a species within its order is:

>Family: *Genus species*

For example, mayflies are the order Ephemeroptera. The mayfly we call the Quill Gordon is Heptageniidae: *Epeorus pleuralis.* The family is capitalized and followed by a colon; the genus and species are italicized. The genus is capitalized but the species is not. In some cases, families are broken down to subfamilies, however the charts show only the family, genus, and species.

When listing several species of the same genus the genus will often be abbreviated and only the species is spelled out. Thus, if the subject were *Epeorus*, you might see *E. pleuralis* and *E. longimanus.*

The plural of "genus" is "genera." The plural of larva is "larvae" (pronounced lar-vee); the plural of pupa is "pupae" (pu—pee). "Species" is both a singular and a plural word. In some fly fishing circles, referring to an insect "specie," without the final "s," is a social blunder equivalent to wearing sweat socks with a tuxedo. "Species" singular is abbreviated "*sp.*" and "species" plural is abbreviated "*spp.*"

In many cases, it is sufficient—for fly fishing—to identify the insect only down to its genus, since the differences between species may be very slight and of no interest to fish or fly fisher. Thus a hatch chart may indicate "*Glossosoma spp.*" to cover the case of all species of *Glossosoma.*

Why Latin? Common names for insects are imprecise and the same name is often used to describe several completely different insects. You soon realize there are a lot of mayflies with blue wings and olive bodies, and people call these Blue Winged Olives. In fact, they may be talking about ten or more species, each of which has a different size and may require different tactics. There is no standardization of common names, and any attempt to do so is doomed from the start. There is simply less confusion when scientific names are used and that is why more flyfishers are using them. Unfortunately, just when you get all the scientific names memorized, some hot-shot entomologist will come up with a new theory about how the species evolved and a whole bunch of the names will change.

In general, good observation skills are of more value than a knowledge of Latin. In fact, it is possible to find two insects of different colors and sizes in the same place at the same time, and they will turn out to be the same species. You may find the trout to be more selective on the color and size differences than on the Latin.

Types of Fly Patterns

Fly patterns are divided into two general categories: imitators and attractors. Imitator patterns closely resemble food that trout eat and stimulate a feeding response. An attractor pattern, on the other hand, is not generally taken by the trout as food, but experience shows that the fly sometimes stimulates a strike response anyway. Common attractor patterns include Royal Coachman, Royal Wulff, and Trude.

When to use attractor patterns. Use attractors when you cannot stimulate a response from the trout with patterns that imitate available, but not actively hatching, food. Page 117 has some guidelines for choosing an attractor pattern.

When **NOT** *to use attractor patterns.* When the hatch is on and trout are actively feeding, you need to match the available food. And you'll have a lot better chance with something other than a Royal Coachman.

Types of Imitator Fly Patterns. Imitator patterns can be classified by the form of food they represent. In general, these are:

Nymph/Larva
Pupa
Emerger
Dry (dun or other adult)
Spinner
Submerged adult
Other

Common examples are shown in Figures 3-8 through 3-12. The types of patterns refer to the life cycle of the insects involved. The fly type referred to here as "emerger" is variously referred to as "cripple," "emerger," "hatching mayfly," "floating nymph," etc. In this book, an "emerger" is a fly that imitates an insect (mayfly or midge) that is in the process of hatching out of its shuck in open water, or a mayfly adult that emerged underwater and is rising to the surface (such as a Quill Gordon). See the *hatching* POV on page 36.

Figure 3-8. *Fly types - Dry flies*

Figure 3-9. *Fly types — Dry flies (rows 1 and 2), spinners (row 3), and submerged adults (row 4)*

Filoplume May
(Mayfly)

Ostrich Baetis
(Mayfly)

Kaufmanns Stone
(Stonefly)

Girdlebug
(Stonefly)

Randalls Dragon
(Dragonfly)

Maribou Damsel
(Damselfly)

Filoplume Damsel
(Damselfly)

Cased Caddis
(Caddis)

Green Rock Worm
(Caddis)

Net-spinning Caddis
(Caddis)

Figure 3-10. *Fly types — Nymph / Larva imitations*

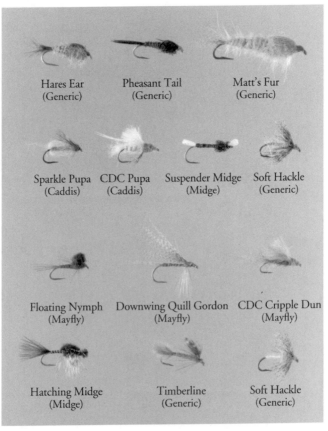

Figure 3-11. *Fly types — Nymph (row 1), Pupa (row 2), Emerger (rows 3 and 4)*

Figure 3-12. *Fly types — Other*

Depth of Presentation

How Deep to Present the Fly

In both rivers and lakes, flies that imitate most aquatic insects should usually be presented either:

On the surface film.

In the surface film.

Under the surface film. (immediately under the film; top 1 inch of water)

Near the surface. (top 12 inches of water)

On the bottom. (bottom 12 inches, or just above the weeds, which is as close as you can get)

Moving. (either up or down, either near the surface or near the bottom)

Scuds, damselflies, and most dragonflies are usually in the top three feet of water. Other aquatic life, like leeches, can be found at almost any depth where trout are found.

How to Achieve the Proper Depth

On the film. Use a floating line and floatant on the fly. If the water is rough, you may need a heavily-hackled or hair wing fly to keep the fly from sinking.

In the film. Use the same techniques as above, but use a fly with little or no hackle so it will sit down in the film. If the fly is sinking, don't put floatant on the leader, as this causes additional drag. Instead, switch to a fly that will float at the right level.

Under the film. Use similar techniques to those above, but the trick is to get the fly to break through the film while not sinking

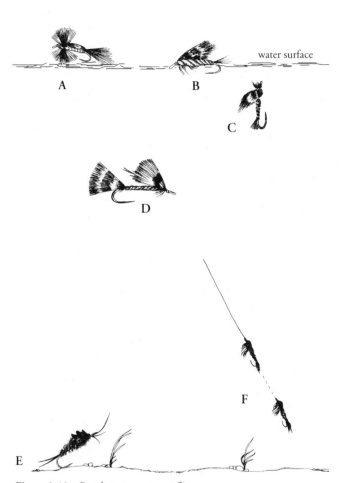

water surface

A

B

C

D

E

F

Figure 3-13. *Depths to present most flies.*
A—*On the film*   C—*Under the film*   E—*On the bottom*
B—*In the film*   D—*Near the surface*   F—*Moving*

more than an inch or two. Spitting on the fly before you cast can help it break the surface tension of the water, then the leader should support it. If it still won't break through, put "mud" or some similar material on the leader near to the fly. When fishing a floating nymph style of fly, dress just the top ball with floatant.

Near the surface. Use floating line, or an intermediate line if there is not much current. If your fly is not large, it will probably need to be lightly weighted in order to break through the film.

On the bottom. This can be the hardest depth of all to achieve, especially if you are fishing a fast river. See page 191 for a description of how to cast a heavy fly. Some ways to achieve depth are:

• Use a weighted fly. Cast far enough upstream so the fly has time to sink to the right depth before it reaches the fish. Mending the fly line so the line/leader knot lands above the point where the fly entered the water will help the fly sink faster. (See page 185.)

• To sink a small fly quickly, put it on a dropper with a heavy fly on the point. (See page 194 for how to rig up a dropper.)

• Put a removable split shot or other lead on the leader about 12-18 inches from the fly. Always use removable lead, such as flat, twist-on strips, split shot with wings, or soft lead. In some states, putting lead on the leader violates fly-fishing only regulations.

• Use a sink tip line in rivers. The sink tip will get the fly down, but the floating portion of line will give you some line control. As with a weighted fly, cast far enough upstream for the fly to reach the right depth by the time it gets to the fish. Sink tip lines can be a problem because the current is much slower on the bottom. This creates a belly in the sink tip due to its extra thickness, and results in drag. Usually a floating line with a long leader and a weighted fly gives a more natural presentation.

• Use a full sinking line in lakes. Sink rates vary with different lines. Count down until you reach the desired depth.

When you are fishing a sinking or sink tip line and are retrieving the fly as part of the presentation, you will need to balance the sink rate with the retrieval speed to stay at the same depth. Experimentation with each combination of line and retrieval technique is the only reliable way to achieve this.

Presentation Tactics for Rivers

Upstream dry. Cast upstream—either directly above you or across the river. As the fly comes back to you, pull in loose line so you can strike quickly if you get a rise. When pulling in line, be careful not to move the fly. Face your body in the direction in which you are casting: if you are casting straight upstream, face upstream; if you are casting across stream, face the direction your fly will land. Watch your fly. If it disappears in swirl, raise your rod tip and tighten your fly line.

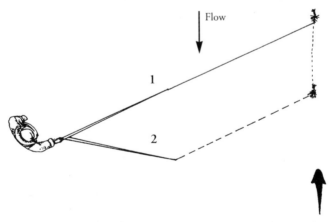

Figure 3-14. *Upstream dry or emerger. Pull in slack line and move rod as fly drifts back to you, but don't move fly.*

Upstream emerger. Similar to upstream dry except the fly is in the top few inches of water. When fishing emergers, an occasional slight twitch of the fly can entice trout. Watch the line-leader junction. If it bounces or jerks, strike. Many anglers strike too often when fishing just subsurface. This causes the fly and fly line to rip through the water and frighten the trout.

Downstream dry. Face downstream, and cast straight downstream from you. As you release the cast, bring the rod back to you. This will give you some slack line. You can also give yourself some slack by wiggling the rod tip as you release the cast. Follow the fly downstream with the rod to maintain contact. Sometimes you can feed extra line through the guides and extend the drift, but this is hard to do without causing drag. With spooky fish, such as on a spring creek, this may be the only presentation that works because the fly

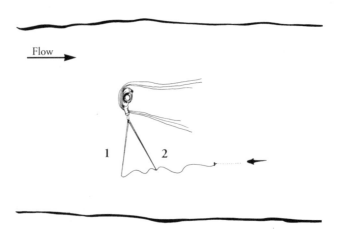

Figure 3-15. *Downstream dry or emerger. Rod is upstream as fly settles* (1), *then is moved downstream to allow fly to drift naturally to trout* (2).

reaches the fish before the line and leader, and drag is minimized.

Note: Because the line is directly below you, you can pull the fly right out of the fish's mouth when you strike; therefore wait just a fraction of a second longer before striking so that the fish has time to close its mouth on the fly.

Downstream emerger. Similar to downstream dry, but you are fishing the top few inches of water. See the comment above about when to strike.

Deep nymph on a tight line. Cast upstream with a short line—around 15 feet, including leader, past the rod tip. As soon as the fly hits the water, mend line upstream so all the line and leader is upstream from the fly. As the fly comes back to you, keep a tight line by lifting the rod. Lower the rod as the fly passes you. Watch the line where it moves through the water. If it hesitates or stops, lift the rod enough to move the fly—you won't need to move it much to hook a fish because you have a tight line. Cast several

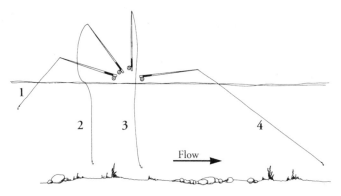

Figure 3-16. *Deep nymph on a tight line. Cast upstream (1). Mend line so line and leader are upstream from fly (2). Raise the rod as the fly drifts to you (3), lower rod as fly passes you (4).*

times to cover the breadth of reachable water in front of you. Then take two or three steps upstream and start again. See page 191 for techniques for casting a heavy fly.

Note: With this tactic, knowing when to strike is an intuition that is developed only with practice.

Deep nymph with an indicator. This is much different than the technique described above, even though it is often done with the same flies in the same water. Put a strike indicator—one that floats—on your leader 6 to 8 feet from the fly. Cast upstream. Ideally, the fly and indicator should be in a straight line, parallel with the current; mend line if possible. As soon as the indicator sinks, jerks, moves sideways, or does anything that looks unnatural, pull your rod downstream hard, maybe even hauling in line with your free hand. With this presentation there is always more slack than you realize, so you need to move a lot of line in order to move the hook 1/2 inch (which is all that is necessary to hook a fish). You can cast farther with this presentation than with the preceding one, but 30 feet is about the limit; beyond that distance you cannot detect the subtle motions of the indicator that show a strike. See page 191 for techniques for casting a heavy fly.

Note: A very heavy fly such as a stonefly nymph can easily sink your indicator if the water is deep or slow. If this happens move the indi-

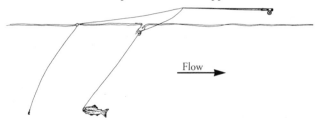

Figure 3-17. *Deep nymph with an indicator. The indicator will sink if the fly is stopped by a fish (or a rock, log, etc.).*

cator up the leader, lengthening the leader, if necessary. If the indicator sinks it is difficult to detect the movements that indicate a strike.

Wet fly swing. Cast straight across stream in slow water, or at more of an angle (up to 60 degrees) in faster water. Mend upstream or downstream so that the fly moves across the river at the same speed it moves down the river. Let the fly swing until it is directly below you, then let it hang there for a few seconds before casting again. The key to this presentation's effectiveness is that the fly moves downstream at the same speed it moves across stream. Throughout your fly's drift, watch the water in the vicinity of the fly. You are looking for a bulge in the water, or a dorsal fin that breaks the surface. Don't strike! Fish will usually hook themselves. When this happens, raise your rod tip. To cover the water, cast a short line first,

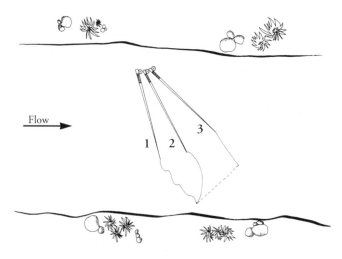

Figure 3-18. *Wet fly swing. Cast across stream (1). Mend downstream (2) to make fly move across stream at same speed as it moves downstream (3).*

and lengthen each cast by two or three feet. When you reach the limit of your casting, take a step or two downstream and cast again.

Skating (dry fly swing). This is a downstream presentation like the wet fly swing, except it is done with a heavily hackled dry fly, such as an elk hair caddis or a dry stonefly that will ride on top of the water. You are imitating an adult caddis that is running across the water, or a stonefly that is being blown across by the wind.

Rising nymph. Cast upstream and allow the fly to sink, which will take longer than you think. Control slack line by gathering it back to you as the fly drifts towards you. When you think you are on the bottom and near a fish, lift the rod slowly to bring the fly to the surface. This tactic is most useful when you know, or strongly suspect, where a trout is laying. It is not a good searching tactic.

Dapping. Use very little line past the rod tip. Hide behind a bush or similar obstruction and drop the fly in front of a fish. Gently bounce it up and down so as to imitate an insect touching the water repeatedly (as when ovipositing).

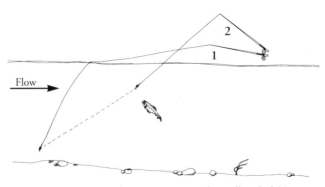

Flow

Figure 3-19. *Rising nymph. Cast (1). Raise rod or pull in slack (2) to make nymph rise.*

If you are casting upstream, you should walk upstream when you are ready to move to new water. Similarly, if you are casting downstream, your progress will be downstream. This way you are always moving onto fresh water.

Presentation Tactics for Lakes

Rising nymph. Use a sink tip line with a 9 foot leader, or a floating line with a weighted fly and long (12-25 foot) leader. Cast and allow the fly to sink, but not necessarily to the bottom. Pull it in steadily. You are imitating a nymph or pupa rising from the bottom to the surface.
Note: vertical retrieves like this seem to work especially well with brook trout.

Midge pupa. Midge pupae are very important food in lakes. They often hatch at dusk, and fish will begin to rise all around you taking the tiny midge pupae and ignoring your big dry fly or

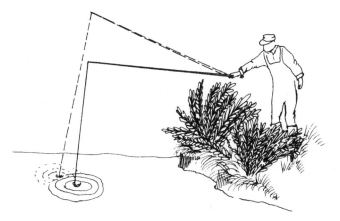

Figure 3-20. *Dapping to imitate ovipositing adult.*

streamer. When this happens, keep a stiff upper lip and tie on a midge pupa. Prepare your fly and leader, as discussed on page 98, for achieving a depth just under the surface film. Your fly should break the film and hang vertically just below the surface. Let it sit there for a minute, then sloooowly pull it towards you to bring it up. Some flyfishers tie on up to 3 midge pupae at once. They let two hang from the leader and tie the third at the end.

With this technique you can experiment with different sizes or colors and see which works best. Or you can fish 3 identical flies to increase our odds. You may also increase your frustration. This rig is a bear to cast without tangling, and tangled leader in fading light with big fish rising all around you may not be your idea of a satisfying fishing experience.

Count down and retrieve. Use sink tip or full sinking line. Cast and count until the fly reaches the proper depth, then retrieve in the manner appropriate to the food type (see pages 68-71 and 110-112). Count to what? Count to whatever depth you catch fish at. If you start hooking bottom or picking up weeds, you've gone too far and should count down a little less. Vary the depth until you find one that works. Keep in mind that as your fly and line sink, they will come closer to you, so if you are trying to hit a certain spot you will need to cast past it. The retrieval rates shown in the charts are a good place to start, but if you get no results, vary the speed of the retrieve. Sometimes a super fast retrieve is the only thing that will induce a strike.

Chuck and sit. Cast a dry fly and let it sit. If nothing happens after a minute, cast to a different place. When you spot a cruising fish,

Figure 3-21. *Multiple pupa rig.*

cast ahead of it so the fly can settle before the fish arrives. If you spot a rise and the fish is not cruising, cast to the center of the rise. During a hatch it is often better to wait until you see a rise, then immediately cast to it.

Dry flies are usually much less important than wet flies in lakes. Even when the fish are taking surface food, they are often just as happy with a pupa or nymph. There are exceptions, such as when damselflies are ovipositing. A dry fly presentation in a lake has to be more delicate than in most rivers because a lake is calmer. In a river, the fly goes whizzing by in the current, and a fish has to make a quick decision. In a lake, the line, leader, and fly sit where they land and are exposed to unlimited scrutiny by naturally suspicious trout.

Lift and settle. Cast a sinking fly on a floating line and let it settle to the desired depth. Slowly retrieve enough line to bring it up a few feet. If there is no take, let it sink again and repeat. This is really a repetitive version of the *rising nymph*, except you don't come all the way to the surface. This presentation is useful for imitating the pre-hatch behavior of some insects like *Hexagenia* and *Callibaetis*.

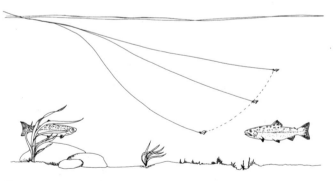

Figure 3-22. *Count down and retrieve. Cast past desired fishing area, let fly settle to depth, then retrieve by stripping in line.*

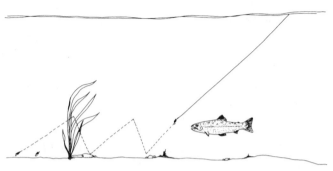

Figure 3-23. *Lift and settle. Let fly settle to depth, then raise it a few feet. Then let it settle. Repeat several times.*

Slow retrieve. A very slow retrieve of a nymph or pupa just under the surface can be effective. Sometimes it imitates the behavior of emerging insects, while at other times it may just focus a trout's attention on your fly. Use a floating or intermediate line, and an unweighted or lightly weighted fly. Make sure the fly pierces the surface film. Retrieve very slowly—about an inch or two of line each second. Slow retrieves of midge pupae and *Callibaetis* nymphs can be deadly in lakes. During slow retrieves, most strikes will be subtle and will feel like a slight hesitation or "stickiness." When this happens, bring your rod up sharply.

Other Common Aquatic Foods

Other fish. Trout eat other fish. In lakes, use a count-down-and-retrieve presentation similar to that for leeches. In rivers, you may also use a wet fly swing presentation. Bait fish usually occur at any depth in the top 15 feet of water.

Scuds. Scuds are fresh water crustaceans (like shrimp) that are often found in lakes and in slow-moving water. They prefer shore-

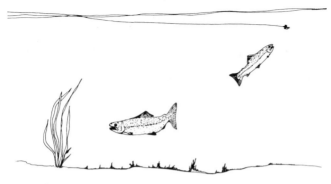

Figure 3-24. *Slow Retrieve. Like count down and retrieve, but usually done near surface.*

line areas, and do poorly in lakes where the water level changes often. Scuds like weed beds and avoid bright light. They prefer to swim in the top 3 feet of water and are rarely found in deep water.

Scud patterns should be fished with a count-down-and-retrieve presentation, usually in the top three feet of water.

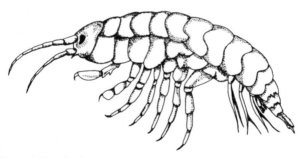

Figure 3-25. *Scud*

Other Common Aquatic Foods

Retrieve them with uneven, erratic strips.

Leeches. Leeches are present in almost all lakes and in the slow parts of rivers. They are generally black or brown. Most North American species will not suck your blood, so forget about that scene with Humphry Bogart pulling the African Queen through the swamp. Leeches are generally nocturnal, but some come out in the day time and are readily taken by fish. Fishing leeches at midnight under a full moon can be amazingly productive. However, not all states allow fishing that long after sundown, and fishing in the dark is not everyone's idea of fun.

Fish leeches with a count-down-and-retrieve presentation. You will need to experiment to find the right depth; anywhere between the surface and the weed tops may work. Strip in about 24 inches of line in 2 seconds, with a slight pause between strips.

Other food. Trout eat terrestrial bugs such as grasshoppers, ants, beetles, spiders, or bees if they are available. These are usually fished like dry flies, with an occasional twitch that looks like a struggling critter. Trout also eat snails, but are generally not selective about them and will take other flies cast near them. Flies imitating snails have not yet been proven to work well.

Canned corn, green marshmallows, and Velveeta™ cheese are not natural trout foods, and no fly patterns or presentations for them will be discussed here.

Figure 3-26. *Leech*

Choosing a Fly and Presentation

Deciphering Feeding Activity

When you see actively rising fish—not just an occasional splash, but lots of fish rising repeatedly—you need to find out four things before you can choose a fly with confidence. They are, in order of importance:

1. *The POV the trout are focusing on.*

2. *The size of the insect.*

3. *The order of the insect.*

4. *The color of the insect.*

Fortunately the trout often give you some clues you need to determine the right POV and insect order.

Clues to POV—Rise Forms

If you see splashy rises, or rises that leave a bubble in the rise ring, the correct depth is probably *on the film,* and the POV is either *drying dun, accident,* or *ovipositing.*

If you see swirls on the water but no splash or bubble in the rise ring, they are probably taking nymphs or pupae just under the surface. The POV is *under the film* or *rising.*

If you see quick splashy rises but no insects on the surface, they may be taking caddis pupae. The POV is *under the film* or *rising.*

If you see porpoising fish (head, then back, then tail) they are probably taking nymphs or pupae subsurface. The POV is *under the film.*

If you see drifting adults suddenly disappear in a swirl, the POV is probably *drying dun* (if you are in a mayfly hatch), or *ovipositing.*

Other Clues

If there are clouds of tiny insects in the air very close to the water's surface, it is probably a midge hatch. The most likely POV and depth are *under the film.*

If there are drifting insects on the surface that look like little sailboats—mayfly hatch. If trout are taking them, the POV is *drying dun* and the depth is *on the film.*

If many insects are flying about and occasionally dipping to the surface, look for spent insects on the surface (they can be hard to see). If trout are feeding on them the POV is *ovipositing* and the depth is *on the film.*

If there are many mayflies with their wings spread out flat on the water, this is a spinner fall; if trout are taking them, the POV is *ovipositing* and the depth is *in the film.*

If your water has fish recently released from a hatchery, they will tend to be surface feeders and prefer a dry fly fished *on the surface.*

If the wind is blowing and you see rises downwind or downstream from overhanging trees and other vegetation, the POV could be *accident,* especially if you are in a region with heavy caddis or stonefly populations. The depth is *on the film.*

In riffles (where the surface tension of the water is broken and the emerging insect is less likely to get trapped under the film) a hatching mayfly is more likely to be taken on the surface as a *drying dun.*

In calm, flat water, hatching mayflies are more likely to be taken *under the film,* because the surface tension is stronger and they get trapped there.

On hot days, when the duns can dry their wings quickly and fly off, the POV for mayflies is more likely to be *under the film.*

On damp days it takes longer for mayflies to dry their wings, and the POV is more likely to be *drying dun.*

In lakes, trout are much more likely to focus on *swimming, rising,* and *under the film* POVs.

Choosing a Fly

Choosing an Imitative Fly —
When Fish are Obviously Feeding

Pick a fly type consistent with your best guess of POV. If your choice is a dry fly, match the fly pattern to the water type. In other words, use a heavily hackled high floating fly for rough water, and a fly with little (or no) hackle for slow or still water. In general, choose a fly with the least amount of hackle that will allow it to float. You can use a pair of small scissors (I use the ones on my Swiss Army knife) to clip hackle off a fly on the spot.

A

B

Figure 3-27. *Pick dry flies by type of water.*
A—*Heavy hackled, hair wing fly for rough water.*
B—*Little or no hackle for flat, quiet water.*

Match size from the sample you have taken. Measure the sample with a ruler, or lay the sample next to your fly choice and compare the body lengths. Too many anglers make a quick estimate without comparing their fly to the real thing; usually they select a fly that is one size too big. If you cannot get a sample, make a guess based on what you see on the water, and be prepared to change it if it doesn't work.

Match the order from the sample, or other clues. If you still aren't sure, use a generic fly like an Adams (dry), or Pheasant Tail or Hare's Ear (wet).

Match the color from the sample. Look really close, using a hand lens if you have one. If you aren't sure of the color, start with a generic color like gray. If that doesn't work, try a lighter color, then a darker. Color is the least important (but sometimes still critical) choice.

If you really don't know what to do, see the next two sections.

Choosing an Imitative Fly — When Fish are NOT Obviously Feeding

If no fish are rising, match the largest or most abundant food type you have found (see Chapter 5). "Match" means size, stage, general appearance, and color—in that order.

If You Really Don't Have a Clue:

For a dry fly, use an Adams.

For a nymph, use a brown hares ear or pheasant tail.

In lakes, use a brown or black leech or wooly bugger, or an olive damsel.

For a streamer, use a muddler.

For wet flies, pick a color that comes close to the color of the underwater vegetation.

For dark days, night fishing, or deep water, use black or purple since the silhouette becomes more important than color in this case.

If it is a very bright day on a lake, a bright, flashy streamer may work.

In small, clear creeks with less than two feet of water, use a dry fly or a soft hackle.

Choosing an Attractor Fly

When a hatch that usually happens doesn't on the day you are there, pick an attractor of the same size as the insect that should have hatched.

Pick a fly color that enhances the available light: red at dawn and dusk; green in a forested area; or reflected light colors, such as gold.

Pick a large fly for rough water.

Go for contrast with surrounding environment.

FOUR

Aquatic Insects

Under the water there is a whole world of living, eating, and being eaten. This miniature world is the link in the food chain that sustains the trout. Little insects turn into adults that leave the world of water for open air and sunshine, search out a mate, and then die and are eaten by trout. The whole cycle of sexual maturation, one quick mating, then death and devourment can happen in as little as a few hours.

This chapter will ignore the obvious moral lessons that can be derived from this life cycle and will concentrate on the scientific facts as they apply to fly fishing. The next section discusses general aspects of aquatic insects. Following sections discuss in general terms the primary aquatic insect orders of interest to flyfishers. Pages 90-91 discuss scientific naming conventions and other insect lingo.

General Information

Aquatic Insect Stages

Aquatic insects go through distinct stages of development with different appearance and behavior at each stage. This process is called metamorphosis, and there are two types of interest to flyfishers:

Complete metamorphosis. The stages are egg, larva, pupa, adult.

Incomplete metamorphosis. The stages are egg, nymph, adult.

Caddisflies and midges go through complete metamorphosis. Mayflies, stoneflies, damselflies, and dragonflies go through incomplete metamorphosis. These stages are discussed below.

Pre-Adult

Nymphs and larvae live underwater. Some, like damselfly nymphs, swim about in search of food. Others, like many caddisfly larvae, crawl among rocks. Still others burrow in mud and silt.

Insects have their skeleton on the outside, and as the nymph or larva grows, the old skeleton becomes too small, splits and falls away, revealing a newer, bigger skeleton underneath. The process is called "molting."

Emergence

When the nymphs of a species mature, the adult must get above the surface of the water and mate. Some nymphs float to the surface where the nymphal skeleton splits one more time, and a winged adult emerges, dries its wings, and flies off in search of the insect equivalent of a singles bar. Other nymphs crawl out of the water onto rocks, sticks, or vegetation, where the winged adult then emerges and flies off. For other species, the adult emerges underwater, and the adult floats to the surface.

Larvae go through a stage that nymphs do not. The larva builds a shelter and seals itself inside until it changes into a pupa. This is a familiar process: it is the same as the cocoon stage of the butterfly. The mature pupa cuts itself free from its shelter, floats or swims to the surface, and the adult emerges out of the pupal skin.

Flyfishers often talk about newly emerged adults "drying" their wings. Actually, the insect is expanding its wings, pumping them up like a balloon, with blood pressure. The amount of time this process takes ranges from near instantaneous (with caddisflies) to almost two hours (with dragonflies).

Adults

Mayfly adults go through one additional change, molting their skin once more to become sexually mature spinners. No other aquatic insects goes through this additional molt. Mayflies live a very short time as adults—from two hours to a couple of days. When they mate, the females come back to the water to lay eggs (oviposit) and often fall into the water dead, or nearly so. They are taken at this stage by trout.

Other insects, like caddisflies and stoneflies, can live for several weeks after emergence. This longer lifetime, most of which is spent in streamside vegetation, combined with their clumsy flying makes caddisfly and stonefly adults available to trout for weeks between emergence and ovipositing. Dragonflies and damselflies also have long lives as adults, but they are excellent fliers and are rarely vulnerable to trout until they come back to oviposit.

Mayflies
(Order Ephemeroptera)

Not the Only Bug in the Brook

On many trout streams mayflies are the dominant aquatic insects that trout eat. Fly fishing authors have traditionally focused on mayflies largely because mayflies were the dominant insects on their streams. Suppose fly fishing evolution were reversed, developing in the western U.S., then exported to the Catskills, and then to Britain. There would then be a great deal of literature about caddisflies and stoneflies, and maybe some about mayflies, too.

The fact is, in some parts of North America mayflies are not the dominant insect. However, fly fishing literature and folklore has focused on mayflies and mayfly tactics, and this sometimes gives rise to myopic thinking about other insect orders.

A proper understanding of mayflies includes not only a knowledge of the insect order itself, but of how mayflies differ in habit and habitat from other insect orders. Anglers will then understand how and when to adjust their fishing to different situations, and will probably find their mayfly fishing is richer for it.

Selective Feeding and Mayflies

There are relatively few species of mayflies (about 570 compared to over 1,200 caddisfly species, and more than 5,000 Diptera just in North America), but mayflies are very prolific and have a short adult lifespan. This is why trout are so selective with mayflies where they are abundant. Since trout are creatures of habit, and there are relatively few mayfly species on the water at any one time, the trout get into a pattern of feeding on just one or two species for several weeks at a stretch. They know what they are looking for and will reject anything that doesn't look like it.

This selectivity has lead to the development of specific fly patterns for many mayfly species. Each pattern exploits the key features that trout look for in the mayfly species that is featured in the day's menu.

Mayfly Life Cycle (Incomplete Metamorphosis)

Nymphs. Nymphs live in the water, either on the bottom among the rocks, burrowed into silt, or swimming.

Emergence. Most mayflies emerge in open water, but nymphs of some species crawl out on vegetation to emerge. Some species

Mayflies (Order Ephemeroptera)   121

actually emerge underwater, and the adults swim to the surface. When emerging in open water, mayflies must first break through the surface film, then crawl out of the nymphal shuck to dry (really, expand) their wings. For all species, each phase of emergence makes it vulnerable (or not vulnerable) to trout in a different way, and a different imitation and tactic is required for each phase.

Duns. Adults that emerge in open water will rest briefly on the surface while their wings dry. Mayfly adults are called "duns" just after they emerge. They will shed their skin (molt) one more time and become sexually mature "spinners".

Spinners. Spinners are adults that have molted from the dun stage. Their bodies are shinier than duns, and their wings are shiny and transparent. Spinners are sexually mature. They mate and the females lay eggs and die. Trout focus on female spinners since they are most likely to return to the water. Spinners of some species oviposit from above the water and therefore are not available to trout unless they die on the surface. Spinners generally fly upstream from their hatch point to oviposit. When a spinner expires on the water it usually lays sprawled out flat, with the wings outstretched.

Male spinners are generally smaller than females. You are more likely to find males on land or in a spider web. Since they may appear different than the females, choosing a fly based on what you find in a spider web can be a mistake.

Other Characteristics of Mayflies

When hatches start. A good rule of thumb is that mayflies tend to hatch at the most pleasant time of day: midday in early and late season when the weather is cooler, or morning and evening in summer when the weather is hotter. "Most pleasant" is a relative term. The author once fished a *Baetis* hatch in February with snow on the bank and ice in the rod guides; but it was at the most pleasant (least frigid) time of day that the hatch started.

Color of Mayflies. The colors of mayfly adults can vary within a single species and sometimes can even depend on how hot it is that day. Sometimes duns will get noticeably darker as soon as they leave the shuck. Thus, knowing the species is not a reliable guide to choosing a fly color.

Telling when a nymph is mature. When mayfly nymphs are mature and near ready to hatch, their wing pads will appear dark brown or black. If the whole nymph is naturally dark brown or black (as many are), you can judge their maturity from the size of the wing pads and how fully developed they appear, or there may be a line along the back of the nymph. Knowing if the nymphs are mature is useful because it tells what is about to hatch.

Types of Mayflies

There are four general categories of mayflies. Chapter 5 describes how to identify the different types and genera of mayflies.

Crawlers. Crawler nymphs crawl about the bottom in search of food and often lose their grip—and are eaten by waiting trout. Crawler genera include *Attenella, Danella, Drunella, Ephemerella, Serratella, Leptophlebia, Paraleptophlebia,* and *Tricorythodes.*

Swimmers. These nymphs swim in slower water and along shoreline vegetation in search of food. This makes them generally available to trout. Mayfly genera that are swimmers include *Callibaetis, Baetis, Diphetor, Pseudocloeon, Ameletus, Isonychia,* and *Siphlonurus.* The first four emerge in open water, but the latter three emerge on above-water objects.

Clingers. Clinger nymphs hold tightly to the bottom. They are so good at this that they rarely lose their grip and are thus seldom available to trout until emergence. Clinger genera include *Cinygmula, Rhithrogena, Stenonema, Epeorus, Heptagenia,* and *Leucrocuta.*

Burrowers. These live in muddy bottoms in slow or still water. Because they are buried in the mud most of their lives, they are not usually taken by trout until they emerge. Burrower genera include *Ephoron, Ephemera, Hexagenia, Litobrancha,* and *Potamanthus.*

Stoneflies (Order Plecoptera)

The large stoneflies of the West, like the Salmonfly and the Golden Stonefly, are often associated with large trout. But there are stonefly species other than these giants, and most free-flowing streams in North America have stoneflies. Some of the small, winter-hatching varieties provide excellent fishing for adventurous anglers.

Stonefly Life Cycle (Incomplete Metamorphosis)

Nymphs. Nymphs of larger species live in fast, riffled sections of rivers. They crawl among the rocks and rubble of the river bottom, usually where the rocks (and hence the spaces between them) are bigger. Nymphs of the giant stonefly (salmonfly) take three years to mature. Some smaller species live in slower water among debris and leaf packs, and some even live in the ground under the river itself.

Since large stonefly nymphs live in water with lots of oxygen, the best places to fish an imitation is just downstream from a riffle as the water gets quieter or deeper, or in faster water that is more than a foot deep. The trout tend to wait in the quieter, safer water for stoneflies nymphs to be brought down to them. The best tactic is a nymph fished deep (See pages 103-105).

Prime time for fishing stonefly nymphs is 2-3 weeks prior to emergence. This is when the nymphs are starting to migrate to shore, and many are knocked loose. At this time of year, trout will congregate in the prime water and feed voraciously on drifting nymphs. However, in areas where large stoneflies are numerous trout will eat them all year long and may be particularly focused on them in the fall when most major hatches are over.

Emergence. At maturity, stonefly nymphs migrate to shore and crawl out on shore vegetation to emerge, hence they are not available to fish during emergence.

Adults. Unlike many species of mayflies, no stoneflies emerge in open water. During the hatch period, however, adults are available to trout when they either blow off streamside vegetation into the water, or when the females come back to oviposit on the surface. Thus, prime areas for fishing dry stoneflies are under trees or next to grassy banks in the afternoon, and in open water in the evening when the females begin ovipositing.

Stonefly adults live much longer than mayflies, so their period of availability can last for weeks after the actual emergence.

Midges and Craneflies (Order Diptera)

In many lakes, midge pupae are critically important insects to trout and to flyfishers, particularly at dusk. They can also be very important in sections of rivers, especially in slow stretches and backeddies.

Midge and Cranefly Life Cycle (Complete Metamorphosis)

Larvae. Like caddisflies, midge and cranefly larvae have adapted to both rivers and lakes, but they live mostly in quiet or still water. Their home is the silt and mud on the bottom, and thus they are rarely available to trout.

Pupae and emergence. Pupation occurs on the bottom. The pupae then drift or swim up to the surface to emerge. Since most of them are quite small, the film is a formidable barrier to them. They may hang just under the film for a long time, especially if the water is calm, as it often is on lakes at dusk when most midge hatches occur. This is their primary point of vulnerability to trout.

When you see lots of trout making head-and-tail rises, and there are clouds of tiny insects over the surface of the water, you are probably in the midst of a midge hatch. Midges make up for their small size with their large numbers, and even the biggest trout will come out to feed on them if the hatch is large. Not all midges are small, however. In the spring on some waters you can fish a midge pupa as big as size 10 all day long. Later in the year you will find mostly small midges, however.

One effective technique in lakes is to use a floating or an intermediate line, and slowly retrieve the midge pupa in the top 12-18 inches of water. Another useful presentation is a vertical retrieve of a midge pupa; brook trout are especially receptive to this.

Midge pupae can be important in rivers at dusk. They rise from slow water and are trapped in food concentrators like backeddies and current seams. Trout will feed selectively and actively on them.

Adults. Adults mate in huge swarms and females return to the water to lay eggs. They are not taken by trout as often as the pupae are, however it is useful to have some imitations on hand such as the Griffith's Gnat. This seems to be more effective at higher elevations, such as mountain lakes.

Cranefly Confusion

Flyfishers usually classify any long-legged, two-winged fly as a "cranefly." This means they usually lump species of the Blephariceridae and Dixidae families in with craneflies (family Tipulidae). The two former families are often more important in running water than are true craneflies.

Dragonflies and Damselflies (Order Odonata)

In many lakes, damselfly nymphs and, to a lesser extent, dragonfly nymphs, are the most important aquatic insect to imitate until the evening hatch of midges. Prime places to fish these nymphs are near weed beds and in areas of downed timber.

Life Cycle (Incomplete Metamorphosis)

Nymphs. Nymphs of both dragonflies and damselflies live in still water, usually in areas of downed timber and weeds, where they feed on other insects. Some damselfly species also live in rivers. Most swim in the water in search of food, although some dragonfly species live on the bottom and wait for food to come to them. Where they occur, swimming damselflies and dragonflies are common trout food the year round.

Emergence. Nymphs migrate to shore or to objects that extend above the surface of the water (vegetation, timber, rocks, etc.). Trout will gorge themselves on the swimming nymphs at these times. Survivors will emerge on above-water objects.

Adults. Since adults emerge on vegetation, they are not generally available to trout. However, trout do take the adult damselflies when they come back to oviposit, and fishing with large dry flies at this time can be very productive.

Types of Dragonflies

Climbers. Climbers actively hunt their prey in open water, and are therefore available to trout. This makes them the most important group of dragonflies to flyfishers. The nymphs favor areas of downed timber and the stems of underwater plants. Genera include *Aeshna* and *Anax*.

Burrowers and sprawlers. These broad, boxy nymphs crawl slowly along the bottom in search of prey, or burrow on the bottom. Because sprawlers stay on the bottom, often in weedy areas, they are not as useful to fisherman as the climber genera, and no charts are included for them. Genera include *Gomphus.*

Caddisflies (Order Trichoptera)

Caddisflies are a highly developed insect order. They have colonized almost all types of water, and with over 1200 very diverse species in North America it is dangerous to make generalizations about them. Flyfishers on caddis-rich water need to always be alert for changing conditions and exceptional situations.

Selectivity and Caddisflies

Trout can be very selective on emerging caddis because there is an abundance of one species at one point of vulnerability at one time. However, trout are not nearly as selective on adult caddis. This is because the adults can live a long time (several weeks) and because many species are available at any given time. During the height of the caddis season trout are seeing so many different species of adults that they rarely get into the selectivity groove we see with mayflies.

Caddis: The Non-Hatch Hatch

With mayflies, both trout and flyfisher interest are focused on the short cycle of emergence and spinner falls. Caddis are different, and thinking of caddis hatches in the same way as mayfly hatches will unnecessarily limit a flyfisher's pleasure.

In many rivers in the West, caddis season goes from July through October. Adults become active as the day warms, and all afternoon they fall or are blown out of trees and into the water.

Some do it as part of ovipositing, but most are just clumsy. Trout wait downstream from overhanging trees and grassy banks to gobble caddis unselectively. This gives the flyfisher hours of productive dry fly fishing, all of which is unrelated to hatch activity and which can continue for weeks after the last major hatch.

Because there can be so many species of caddis dropping into the water each afternoon, the trout are not very selective. Match the size of the most abundant adults, and you're in business. Samples of caddis adults are easy to obtain. Just shake a tree branch and a bunch will fly out and land on you. Pick one up by the wings and measure it against your caddis imitations. (You can always tell an experienced flyfisher; if a bug lands on him he reacts by examining it carefully instead of instantly squashing it.)

Pick a shady spot sheltered by trees, where the water is 2-4 feet deep and has a moderate current. If there are many large boulders on the bottom, so much the better. Watch carefully for feeding trout. Often all you will see is a quiet sip, or a dorsal fin that breaks the surface. You won't see these fish if you are ripping by in a boat or walking along the bank, so pick likely looking water and just start in. The trout will be there, and you will often need to stalk each one carefully. This is trout hunting at its finest.

As the light fades from the water towards evening, the trout will begin feeding more aggressively in mid-river. They will usually take both dry flies and diving caddis. The latter imitates female caddis that oviposit by swimming to the bottom; a "submerged adult" style of fly fished on a wet fly swing is a good tactic.

Caddisfly Life Cycle (Complete Metamorphosis)

Larvae. Caddisfly larvae have adapted to just about every type of water there is, from very fast rivers to lakes. There are over 1200 caddisfly species in North America—more than mayflies and stoneflies, combined.

Many species of larvae build cases to live in, but other species do not build cases. Some of these latter species, such as the genus Rhyacophila, are called "free-living" caddis in reference to their housing (not their life-style) while others are called "net-spinning" caddis.

Larvae of river-dwelling species become dislodged into the drift and are eaten by trout. Thus, you can fish a caddis larva imitation downstream from areas of concentration. Even cased-caddis can be fished, since trout eat the naturals, case and all.

Pupae and emergence. Larvae of all species eventually form a pupal case, seal themselves into it, and change into pupae. The mature pupa cuts itself free from the case. Pupae are generally the same color as the adult.

Pupae of some species float or swim to the surface, where the adult emerges from the pupal skin. During a hatch, these pupae drift momentarily along the bottom of the river, rise quickly to the surface, then hang momentarily under the film.

Pupae of other species crawl to shore and emerge out of the water. While crawling, they may be knocked loose and drift for a while along the bottom.

Thus the two primary points of vulnerability for river-dwelling caddis pupae are at the bottom (all species) and under the film (some species). Lake dwelling species are sometimes taken as they rise.

Adults. The adult emerges quickly from the pupal skin and needs no time for its wings to dry. Thus, a newly emerged adult is not vulnerable to trout and is seldom taken by them. You rarely find newly emerged caddis adults drifting on the river like mayflies.

For some species, the newly emerged adults do not fly away after emergence; they run across the surface towards shore.

Many caddisfly females swim or crawl underwater to lay eggs, and an appropriate wet fly presented on a swing can be very effective. Spent caddis will often be found on the surface after ovipositing. They may also be eaten by trout; a dry fly imitation is best.

Types of Caddisflies

Pages 163-166 show typical caddis larvae for the 5 types of caddis described here.

Saddle-case. Larvae live in dome-shaped cases made from pebbles. The domes stick on top of rocks. Genera include *Glossosoma*.

Micro caddis. Larvae are free living until they near maturity, then they build a simple case. Larvae are generally not important to fish, but pupae are. The primary family is *Hydroptilidae*.

Free-living. Larvae do not live cases, but crawl along the bottom of rivers. Emergence is often at mid-day. The primary genus is *Rhyacophila* (Green Rock Worm).

Net-spinning. Larvae do not build a case, but construct a web net to catch drifting food. Genera include *Hydropsyche* (Spotted Sedge) and *Cheumatopsyche*.

Tube-case. Larvae live in a case made from small pebbles, twigs, or other material. You can check for mature pupae by cutting open the case. If the pupa is mature, its wings will be dark brown or black. The color of the pupa will help you choose the right fly. Genera include *Brachycentrus* (Grannom), *Limnephilus* (over 100 species), and *Dicosmoecus* (October Caddis).

FIVE

Identifying Aquatic Insects

I once fished with a man who identified a certain mayfly as an "LGF". He explained that LGF meant "Little Gray Fellow". Actually, he used a different two-syllable word than "fellow", a word that also started with "f". This man is an excellent flyfisher with decades of experience, but his interest in and knowledge of identifying trout food ended at the LGF level. By the way, he fished circles around me that day.

So the question might naturally occur, "Is all this entomology stuff really necessary?" No, it is not necessary. You can get along without it, and even use the charts in Chapter 3 without being able to identify a single bug. You can get someone else to tell you what to expect, or identify the insects for you; you can even gather samples of the available insect life and choose a fly that matches them in size and color, without knowing what they are. Or you can invest decades of on-the-water fishing time to developing an intuitive feel for how to deal with LGFs when they hatch.

On the other hand, the hatch might be different than you were told to expect. Or nobody knows what to expect. Or you don't have decades of time to invest in LGFs. Your fly fishing may develop to the point where you want to be able to tell—on your own—what bugs are in the water and what it means to your fishing.

Smart Fish

Another reason to learn some basic identification techniques is the increasing sophistication of the trout. In these days of easy travel, hoards of people, insect-literacy, and catch-and-release fishing there are few places you can go and find big, dumb trout. It used to be that a flyfisher could get by with only a Royal Coachman and an Adams—and know no more about insects than to distinguish a caddis from a mayfly—because he was fishing over trout that were major-league ignorant.

On many waters the fishing today is much different than it was even ten years ago. Fishing pressure has educated the trout. They may not speak Latin, but they know what a flyfisher looks like: he looks like trouble. When a trout sees a dozen flyfishers a day for six months of the year, he gets wary and is more careful about what he eats. If it doesn't look just right, he will ignore it. The increasing sophistication of the trout forces the flyfisher to be more sophisticated.

Using This Book to Identify Insects

This section and the next describe the tools you need and how to use them to gather insects. The remainder of this chapter details insect anatomy and the identification process for adults and nymphs.

In this book, identification is taken only to the level necessary to identify which POV chart (pages 44-79) you should use. Thus mayfly nymphs are identified to the genus level, and the remaining insects are identified to a broad category within their order. Identification of mayfly adults below their order is beyond the scope of this handbook.

The Best Identification Strategy

Learn the primary insects on the water you fish. Examine the population in different kinds of water (fast, slow, riffled, etc.), and learn how the insect biomass changes from season to season in these habitats. There are probably only 10-20 insects that make up most of the biomass. Focus on these. Soon you will recognize them easily without a hand lens, know their habits and habitats, and how best to imitate them.

Do You Need to Know the Species?

The passion for identification to the species level was exported from Britain, where there is far less ecological diversity than in North America. This approach is not as useful in eastern North America, and is downright misleading in the West.

Some insect species, like those in the genus *Baetis,* can have several generations in the same year, and the early-hatching species can have a body twice as long as those species that hatch late in the season. Same species, though. Some species of other genera have males and females of different sizes. Same species. Colors can vary depending on water conditions, air temperature, etc. Same species. Emergence dates can vary from one drainage to the next. For the same species. So what good does it do to know the species? In addition, positive identification of the species of many genera is extremely difficult even for a professional with a Ph.D. and a microscope. So there are two problems: it's difficult to reliably determine the species, and it may not do much good anyway.

The behavioral characteristics of aquatic insects that are of interest to flyfishers usually occur at the genus level. If you know the genus you can usually determine the POVs and from that you know the fly types, depths, and the tactics. Knowing the species can give clues as to size and color—the next two most important determinates of fly choice—but these should be determined from actual samples.

The best strategy is to identify insects to their genus (relatively straightforward), then record the location and date of the sample along with the size in millimeters and the color. Odds are you will find the same conditions next year at that spot. This information will do you far more good than knowing the species of the insect. At some point you have to decide if your purpose is to write a scientific treatise ... or catch fish.

Insect Collection and Identification Tools

Nymph net. These can take many forms, including the following:

A mesh that fits over your landing net frame,

A mesh that rolls up on two sticks like the Dead Sea Scrolls (mayfly nymphs are slightly more decipherable),

A "professional" insect collection net,

The foot end of an old pair of panty hose, slipped over your hand like a mitt.

Nymph nets can be used to gather adult insects off the water, too. To gather flying insects you need something more like a small butterfly net. Most fly fishing shops sell several kinds of nymph nets. Scientific supply houses have more elaborate nets, and grocery stores carry panty hose.

Ruler, marked in millimeters. Cheap plastic rulers can be found in the school supplies section of many stores. For convenience, you can cut off everything past 60 mm and just carry the stub end.

Collection vials. These are small plastic bottles with lids. They are used to save insects you have gathered from the water. They are available from scientific supply houses, or ask your pharmacist for some plastic pill bottles. Some people have a collection of bugs like a stamp collection, but even if you don't save the bugs, the collection vials are handy for temporary storage of insects. You can gather a bunch in the water, put them in the vial with water, then take them ashore for identification. Alternatively, you can take the insects home and do your identification work there.

A solution of two parts ethyl alcohol to one part water can be used to preserve most insects; use somewhat more alcohol for larger insects. Use a pencil to write the date and place of collection on a strip of paper, then put the paper in the vial with the insect.

Hand lens. A small, folding hand lens of 10 to 15 power magnification is necessary for a close look at small critters. They are available at scientific supply houses, and are not expensive.

Tweezers. For moving small bugs around. Get stainless steel ones. Few aquatic insects bite, but if you are concerned, handle them with the tweezers.

White plastic lid. This is to put collected insects on for examination. It should be translucent enough to let some light through, and should have sides so you can put a little water in it. (I use the white plastic lid from my collection vials.) Put the bugs you have collected in the lid with a little water. You can even put nymph shucks in the lid with water and they will more closely resemble the original form and give you some clue as to what's going on. If the lid lets some light through it will be easier to see what you have, especially if you are using a hand lens to examine it.

Thermometer. Water temperature plays a role in the behavior of both fish and insects. Most fly shops sell thermometers in metal cases. These respond quickly to temperature changes. One approach is to put the thermometer on a lanyard attached to your vest, drop the thermometer in the water for a short time, then haul it back up.

Monocular (optional). A small monocular can be a very handy tool in your vest. Use it to scan water you can't wade to. Often you can see whether or not there are duns on the water, and maybe even get some clue as to size and color. Many camera shops and outdoor suppliers carry these. The monocular is also nice to have for viewing birds, wildlife, and the activities of other flyfishers.

Discovering What is in the Water

If you are not sure what food lives in the water you are fishing, take a few minutes to find out. Even if you are prepared enough that you know what to expect when you reach the water, it is a good idea to do a reality check.

On shore

Check out trees and bushes alongside the water. Look on the underside of the leaves, since this is where the insects like to hang out.

Shake a few branches and see what flies out.

In the Water

Check the edges of the water for nymph shucks and caddis skins. This can tell you what to expect later in the day.

Pick up some fist-sized or bigger rocks and see what is clinging to them.

Put your nymph net in the top 6 inches of running water and see what you collect in 30 seconds. In still water, sweep the net slowly through the water. Sometimes the pressure of moving water will build up a "cushion" in front of the net that prevents insects from actually reaching the net. If this is happening, tilt the top of the net slightly downstream and lift it slowly. The insects will stick to it as you remove it from the water.

Put a nymph net on the bottom, downstream from you if you are in moving water. Kick up the bottom 6-12 inches in front of the net; let the silt settle, then lift the net and examine the contents. Seining nymphs may be illegal in some states, so check your regulations.

Check your waders when you get out of the water; also, your float tube if you are in a lake. Often you will find various aquatic insects clinging to them.

Look in backeddies and on rocks and logs. You may find dead spinners from the day before stuck there.

Check out submerged logs to see what is clinging to them. This is prime damselfly, dragonfly, scud, and leech habitat. Pick up a piece of wood and turn it over; usually the insects you are looking for will be on the underside, away from the light.

Sweep your nymph net over weed beds and examine the contents. Pick up a piece of aquatic plant and see what is clinging to it.

Ask someone who seems to know what they are doing. (It's amazing how few people will take this step.)

Once You Have Stalked and Bagged the Wily Bug:

Identify the order and type as closely as you can.

Measure it. Measure the body length without the antennae and tails, and compare it to a hook size. Never guess. You will usually be wrong and will pick a fly that is too big.

Note color and general appearance. Do this when the insect is wet if it is a nymph or pupa. Examine the color carefully, up close and preferably with a hand lens. It may surprise you how different the color will appear up close. Refer to figures 5-1 and 5-2 for the nomenclature of basic insect anatomy.

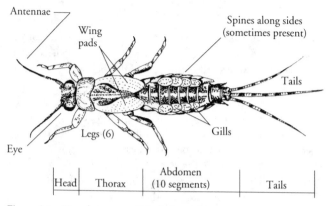

Figure 5-1. *Nymph Anatomy (Mayfly Example)*

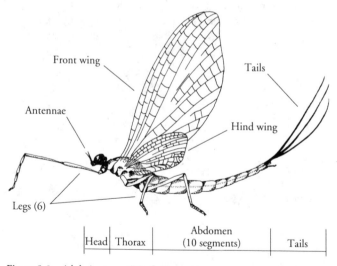

Figure 5-2. *Adult Anatomy (Mayfly Example)*

Discovering What is in the Water   139

Identifying Adults

Use the following illustrations to identify the insect to the correct order. The appropriate charts in Chapter 3 are referenced with each illustration. Identification of adults below the order is beyond the scope of this book.

A simple alternative to identifying mayfly adults to the genus level is to identify the appropriate nymphs. To do this, collect some nymphs and pick out the mature ones that look ready to emerge. They will have fully developed wing pads that will be dark brown or black (of course the whole insect may be dark brown or black to begin with). Also, there may be a line down the middle of the back of the nymph. Identify the mature nymphs and, if they are about the same size as the adults you have just collected, odds are they are the same species as the duns or spinners.

Another alternative to identifying hatching adults is to collect drifting emergers and identify them, if they are nymphs. You will have to kill them first or they will emerge before your eyes!

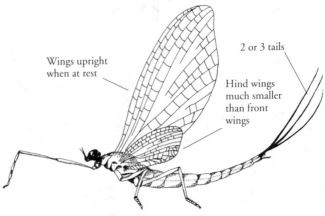

Wings upright
when at rest

2 or 3 tails

Hind wings
much smaller
than front
wings

Figure 5-3. *Mayfly - Charts 1 thru 9*

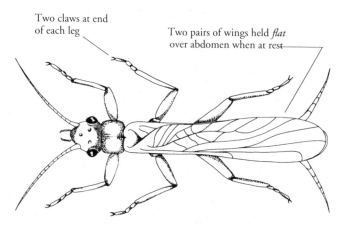

Figure 5-4. *Stonefly - Charts 10 and 11*

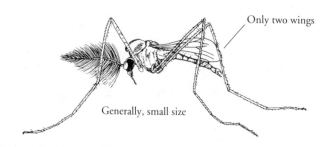

Figure 5-5. *Midge - Chart 12*

Identifying Adults

141

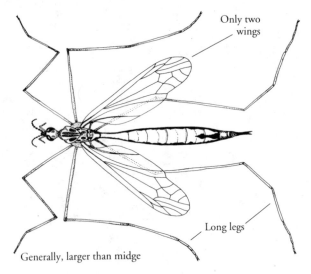

Only two wings

Long legs

Generally, larger than midge

Figure 5-6. *Cranefly - Chart 12*

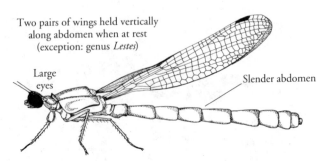

Two pairs of wings held vertically along abdomen when at rest (exception: genus *Lestes*)

Large eyes

Slender abdomen

Figure 5-7. *Damselfly - Chart 13*

Identifying Aquatic Insects

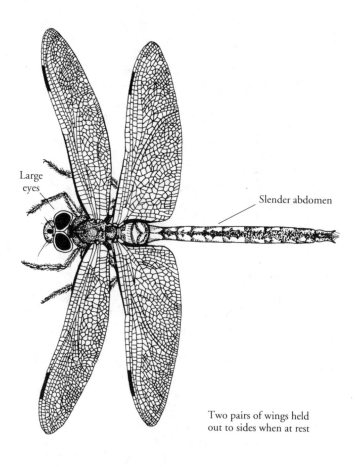

Large
eyes

Slender abdomen

Two pairs of wings held
out to sides when at rest

Figure 5-8. *Dragonfly - Chart 14*

Identifying Adults

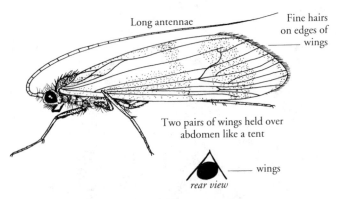

Long antennae

Fine hairs on edges of wings

Two pairs of wings held over abdomen like a tent

wings

rear view

Figure 5-9. *Caddisfly - Charts 15 thru 18*

Identifying Pre-Adult Forms

But soft, what nymphs are these?
A Midsummer Night's Dream

Follow the process outlined below. If the insect looks like one of the pictures, go to the step or chart indicated. Not all insect orders or mayfly genera have been covered—only the more common ones.

These are "quick and dirty" identification techniques and are not scientifically precise. When you are on the water and trout are feeding all around you, you need something that will quickly tell you what to do, or at least get you pretty close. That is the goal of the identification techniques used here; scientific precision is best left for homework. Real entomologists do most of their identification by microscopic examination of the sex organs of the insects, which probably confirms what you always suspected about entomologists.

Hints to the Beginning Bug Identifier

All small mayfly nymphs (about 7 mm long or less) look like they are flat and have a wide head. Flat, wide-headed nymphs are clinger-types, and recognizing this property is an important step in identification of mayfly nymphs. Therefore the general rule should be that if there is any question about a small nymph being a clinger, it probably isn't.

Hold the hand lens close to your eye, then focus by moving the insect close to it. Since the hand lens must be held close to both your eye and the insect, much of the light is blocked out. This makes it difficult to determine the color and characteristics of the insect. Placing it in the white translucent lid helps, since the lid lets in some of the surrounding light. If you have a little flashlight, shining it at the insect may also help.

Gill characteristics are important to mayfly genus identification, but the the little buggers keep wiggling when you put them in water. The best approach may be to kill the insect first, then look at the gills. You can kill the insect by letting it sit out in the sun for a while with no water, or—if this seems cruel and heartless—by placing it in the preservative solution of ethyl alcohol for a minute or so.

Some mayflies have spines along the sides of their abdomens. These may look like gills to the inexperienced eye and be confusing. Gills of live mayfly nymphs usually flutter when in a little water.

If the nymphs all look the same to you, take heart. Learn a little at a time. Take some nymphs home with you and do your identifying there. Start by identifying the order, then move to lower levels. Keep at it, and you will soon get the hang of the process. Over time you will learn what to look for and will become familiar with the insects in your home water. After a while you'll be able to identify most of them without a hand lens.

▶ 1: Mayfly Nymph — Charts 1 - 9

If **NO MATCH**, go to **6**

If **MATCHES**, go to **2 - 5** to identify type
(Swimmer, Clinger, Burrower, or Crawler)

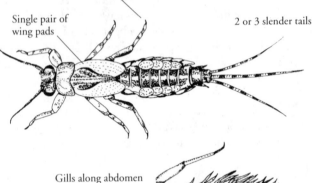

Single claw at
end of each leg

Single pair of
wing pads

2 or 3 slender tails

Gills along abdomen
look like *plates* (above)
or tuning forks (right)

or double plates with
threads at the ends

or double tear drops
with fringes

▶ 2: Mayfly Swimmer — Charts 4 - 6

If **NO MATCH**, go to **3**

If **MATCHES**, go to **2A thru 2F** to identify genus

Generally, when insect is held in the hand,
it will wiggle its abdomen rather than crawl

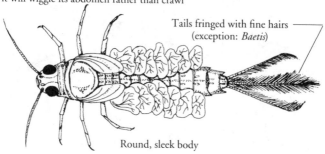

Tails fringed with fine hairs
(exception: *Baetis*)

Round, sleek body

2A: Genera *Baetis* or *Diphetor* — Chart 4

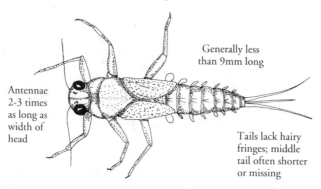

Generally less
than 9mm long

Antennae
2-3 times
as long as
width of
head

Tails lack hairy
fringes; middle
tail often shorter
or missing

2B: Genus *Pseudocloeon* — Chart 4

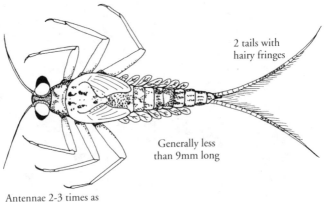

2 tails with
hairy fringes

Generally less
than 9mm long

Antennae 2-3 times as
long as width of head

2C: Genus *Callibaetis* — Chart 5

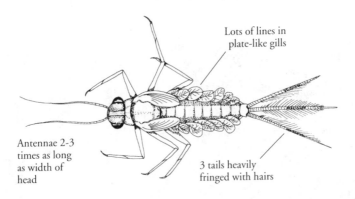

Lots of lines in
plate-like gills

Antennae 2-3
times as long
as width of
head

3 tails heavily
fringed with hairs

2D: Genus *Siphlonurus* — Chart 6

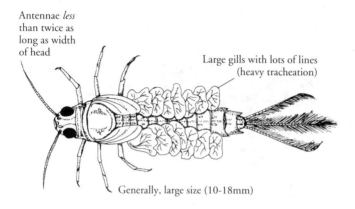

Antennae *less* than twice as long as width of head

Large gills with lots of lines (heavy tracheation)

Generally, large size (10-18mm)

2E: Genus *Isonychia* — Chart 6

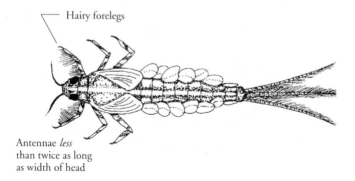

Hairy forelegs

Antennae *less* than twice as long as width of head

2F: Genus *Ameletus* — Chart 6

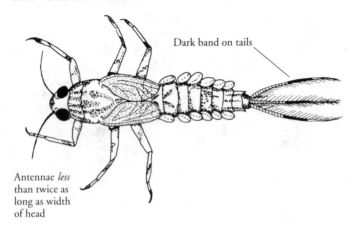

Dark band on tails

Antennae *less* than twice as long as width of head

▶ 3: Mayfly Clinger — Charts 7 and 8

If **NO MATCH**, go to **4**

If **MATCHES**, go to **3A thru 3E** to identify genus

Flat head as wide, or
wider, than abdomen;
eyes more on top of head
than on sides

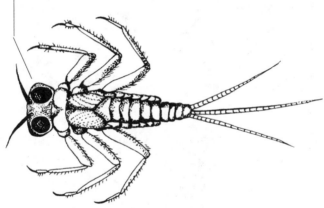

top view

Low profile,
Italian sports car look

side view

3A: Genus *Cinygmula* — Chart 7

Notch in front of head

Detail

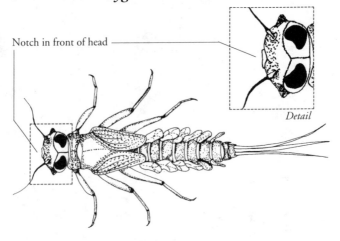

3B: Genus *Stenonema* — Chart 7

Last gill much smaller than others

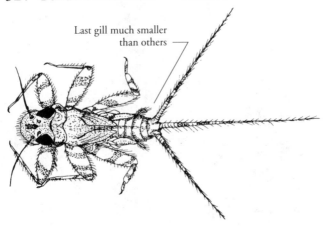

3C: Genus *Rhithrogena* — Chart 7

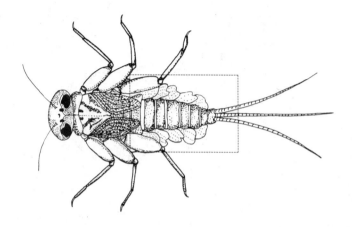

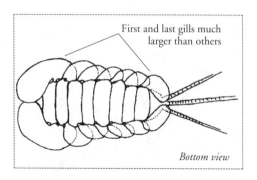

First and last gills much larger than others

Bottom view

3D: Genus *Epeorus* — Chart 8

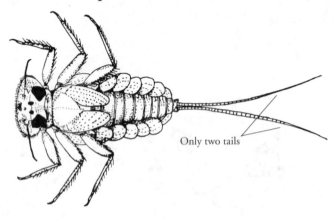

Only two tails

3E: Genera *Heptagenia, Leucrocuta* — Chart 8

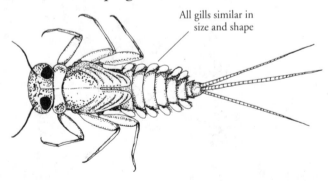

All gills similar in size and shape

▶ 4: Mayfly Burrower — Chart 9

If **NO MATCH**, go to **5**

If **MATCHES**, identify genus from head and tusk shapes

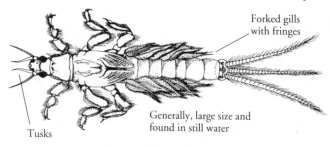

Forked gills with fringes

Tusks

Generally, large size and found in still water

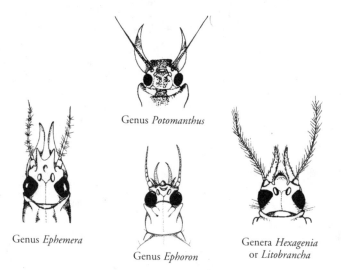

Genus *Potomanthus*

Genus *Ephemera*

Genus *Ephoron*

Genera *Hexagenia* or *Litobrancha*

Note *tusk shapes* and *nose shapes*

▶ 5: Mayfly Crawler — Charts 1 - 3

If you did not find a match in steps 2, 3, or 4,
    you probably have a crawler type mayfly.
    Use **5A - 5D** to identify the genus

5A: Ephemerellidae Family — Charts 1 and 2

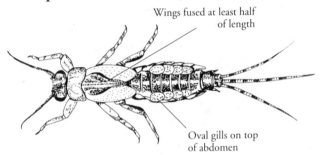

Wings fused at least half
of length

Oval gills on top
of abdomen

Attenella	—	Generally, less than 7mm long; most common in West. **Chart 1**
Danella	—	Generally, around 7mm long; most common in East. **Chart 1**
Drunella	—	First segment of front legs extra wide and serrated in front. **Chart 1**
Ephemerella	—	Last 2/3 of tail fringed with fine hairs. **Chart 2**
Serratella	—	Generally, less than 8mm long; tails relatively hairless. **Chart 2**

5B: Genus *Tricorythodes* — Chart 3

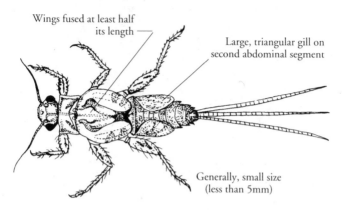

Wings fused at least half its length

Large, triangular gill on second abdominal segment

Generally, small size (less than 5mm)

5C: Genus *Paraleptophlebia* — Chart 3

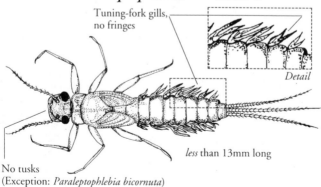

Tuning-fork gills, no fringes

Detail

less than 13mm long

No tusks
(Exception: *Paraleptophlebia bicornuta*)

5D: Genus *Leptophlebia* — Chart 3

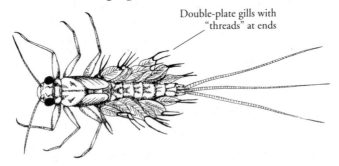

Double-plate gills with "threads" at ends

▶ 6: Stonefly Nymph — Charts 10 and 11

If **NO MATCH**, go to 7

If **MATCHES**, look at underside of insect

If insect has thread-like gills under legs ("hairy armpits"),
       it is a large stonefly   **Chart 10**
       Otherwise, it is a small stonefly **Chart 11**

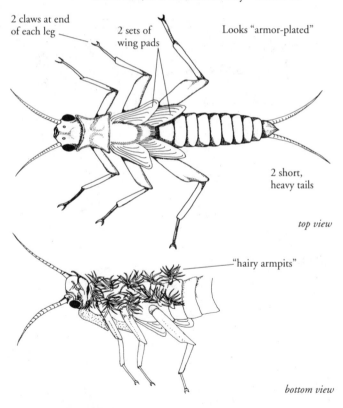

2 claws at end of each leg

2 sets of wing pads

Looks "armor-plated"

2 short, heavy tails

top view

"hairy armpits"

bottom view

▶ 7: Midge / Cranefly Larva — Chart 12

If **NO MATCH**, go to **8**

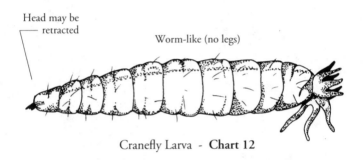

Head may be
retracted

Worm-like (no legs)

Cranefly Larva - **Chart 12**

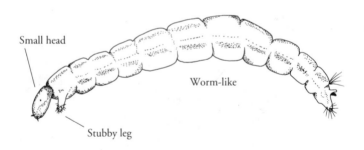

Small head

Worm-like

Stubby leg

Midge Larva - **Chart 12**

If **NO MATCH**, go to **9**

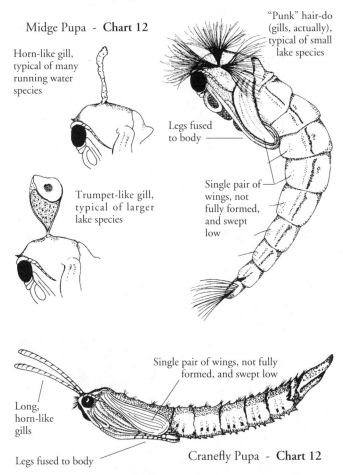

Midge Pupa - **Chart 12**

"Punk" hair-do (gills, actually), typical of small lake species

Horn-like gill, typical of many running water species

Legs fused to body

Trumpet-like gill, typical of larger lake species

Single pair of wings, not fully formed, and swept low

Single pair of wings, not fully formed, and swept low

Long, horn-like gills

Legs fused to body

Cranefly Pupa - **Chart 12**

▶ 9: Damselfly Nymph — Chart 13

If **NO MATCH**, go to **10**

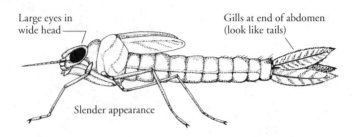

Large eyes in wide head

Gills at end of abdomen (look like tails)

Slender appearance

▶ 10: Dragonfly Nymph — Chart 14

If **NO MATCH**, go to **11**

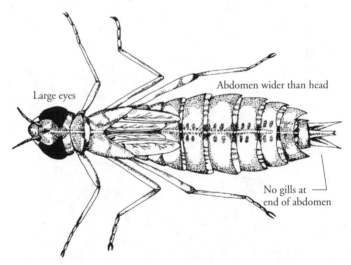

Large eyes

Abdomen wider than head

No gills at end of abdomen

▶ 11: Caddis Pupa — Charts 15 - 18

If **NO MATCH**, go to **12**

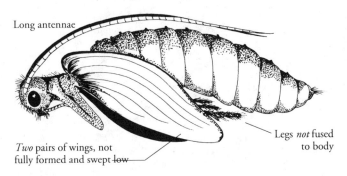

Long antennae

Two pairs of wings, not fully formed and swept ~~low~~

Legs *not* fused to body

▶ 12: Saddle-Case Caddis Larva — Chart 15

If **NO MATCH**, go to **13**

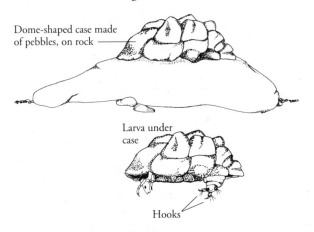

Dome-shaped case made of pebbles, on rock

Larva under case

Hooks

▶ 13: Micro Caddis Larva — Chart 15

If **NO MATCH**, go to **14**

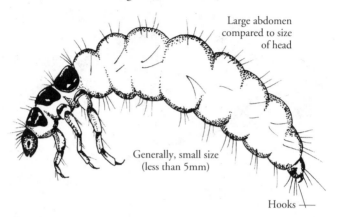

Large abdomen
compared to size
of head

Generally, small size
(less than 5mm)

Hooks

▶ 14: Free Living Caddis Larva — Chart 16

If **NO MATCH**, go to **15**

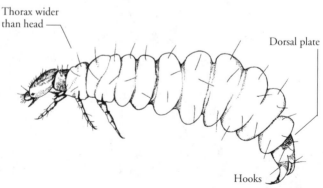

Thorax wider
than head

Dorsal plate

Hooks

If **NO MATCH**, go to **16**

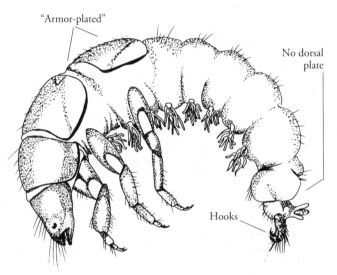

"Armor-plated"

No dorsal plate

Hooks

Head as wide as thorax, or wider

▶ 16: Tube Case Larva—Chart 17 (Rivers)
Chart 18 (Lakes)

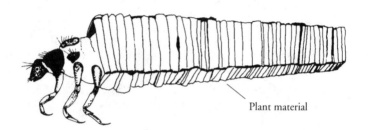

Plant material

Pebbles

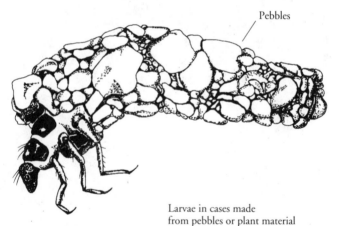

Larvae in cases made
from pebbles or plant material

Cases may be in a variety of shapes

SIX

Other Subjects

This chapter covers miscellaneous subjects that did not fit neatly into the previous chapters.

Trout are both predator and prey, and it is vital to your fly fishing success to understand the implications of this fact. The most important part of being a predator is eating; thus, the feeding behavior of trout is the first topic discussed, beginning on page 169. The most important part of being prey is to avoid being eaten, which means that trout are wary creatures who are sensitive to how you approach them. This is the subject of the section beginning on page 173. Following this, on page 177, you will find details on a special aspect of approaching trout: wading.

We may frequently despair about the quality of our political leaders. Our fly fishing leaders, however, are usually cheaper to purchase and—with the aid of a few instructions—more easily controlled. These are covered beginning on page 181.

If you threw a dry fly into the river all by itself, it would drift naturally. A fish might even eat it. This might provide some satisfaction in fooling the fish, but even more enjoyment will be yours if you are connected to the fly by line and leader. Unfortunately this connection of line and leader can destroy proper presentation of your fly through drag. Drag and how to deal with it is covered beginning on page 185.

If you don't know how to cast yet, you won't learn how from this book. However, some basic points are reviewed and problems areas are discussed beginning on page 189. Following this is a discussion of where to place your casts (page 193).

On page 194 is the true catch-all section: the miscellaneous subjects in the miscellaneous chapter. Nevertheless, there are some important topics in there.

Some days fly fishing seems so easy that you might decide to write your own book. But no matter how good a flyfisher you are, there comes a time when you stare blankly at an inscrutable body of water, and wonder what the heck the fish are doing. Some hints about what to do when nothing works begin on page 198.

Trout are beautiful creatures, superbly adapted to their aquatic world, and they are wonderful fun to pursue with fly fishing fakery. But when you have landed one, let it go safely so it can get on with the business of life. For details on how to do this see page 202.

When you have actually caught something, your first reaction might be pride. The next might be curiosity about what this finny, slimy critter is. Refer to the illustrations beginning on page 205.

A fishing guide would not be complete without a section on knots, so you'll find illustrations of the commonly used ones beginning on page 207. After covering knots to do on the water, it is important to mention a few things *not* to do on the water. See page 210. Finally, you'll find a glossary beginning on page 212, so, even if you got skunked, you can go to a local cafe and speak the lingo like a pro.

Feeding Behavior of Trout

Selective vs. Opportunistic Feeding

At times, trout may feed on only a certain species of insect or other food, and even focus on a single point of vulnerability for that food. This is selective feeding. At other times the same fish may take almost anything that looks edible; this is called opportunistic feeding.

The degree of selectivity can vary depending on the water you are fishing. Some of the situations that tend to create selective feeding are:

Massive hatches of a single species of insect creates very selective feeders. This is often the case with mayflies, and is why many mayfly species have specific fly patterns developed for them.

Slow, clear waters.

Heavy fishing pressure.

If you are not accustomed to fishing over selective trout and are traveling to water that has the above characteristics, you need to be prepared to refine your tactics to accommodate these picky, frustrating fish.

Other Aspects of Feeding Behavior

Multiple hatches. In waters with multiple hatches occurring simultaneously, it is not unusual for a trout in one feeding area to be selective to a different species than a trout in an adjacent area. Usually they focus on the most abundant insect and stage in their territory. Also, trout are creatures of habit. If hatches of different species are overlapping, they will tend to take the species that began hatching earlier in the year.

Early stages of a hatch. During the early stages of a hatch trout may be less selective and take any fly that is the right size, but when the hatch is in full swing they may take only a fly that exactly matches the natural.

Stupefied trout. In areas with large hatches at limited times of the day, trout will often gorge themselves during the hatch, then go to quiet water to digest the meal. They know there will be more later, so almost nothing you can offer will entice them. Like them, you know it will be good later.

Fast water. If there is a major hatch, trout in fast water will wait on the bottom where the current is slower. They will rise to the surface, grab a bug, then go back to the bottom.

Quiet water. Conversely, during a hatch in quiet water, trout will be nearer the surface. This also means that their rises will be less splashy and obvious.

Sparse hatch. If the hatch is sparse, trout may wait on the bottom where they get a wider view of surface insects coming their way. This may affect how you approach and cast to the trout.

Temperature. Temperature can play a big role in feeding behavior. There may be little activity until the water gets up (or down) to a certain temperature. In some cases, insect activity is triggered by the temperature. In other cases, the trout (being cold-blooded) may be too lethargic (if the water is cold) or oxygen deprived (if it is hot) to respond.

Feeding rhythm. Trout in both lakes and rivers will often establish a feeding rhythm. If you spot a feeding fish, time the interval between its rises, and make your presentation such that your fly reaches the fish at the right moment.

Feeding territory. Large trout often establish a feeding territory and keep other fish out of it. The territory with the best protection and most food will be occupied by the most aggressive (usually biggest) trout.

Key Features and Feeding Behavior

Your bait of falsehood takes this carp of truth…
    Hamlet

Trout focus on certain key features of their food possibilities. These may include size, color, motion of legs, dimples of light on the water's surface made by the adult insect's legs, silhouette, type of swimming motion through the water, iridescence, etc. It is not always clear what these key features are, and they can vary from one river or lake to another.

Good fly patterns are often developed for a particular locality and are very effective there because they contain the key features that trout in that location are focused on. However the same patterns may not work as well elsewhere because those trout are focused on a different mix of key features. If a trout doesn't find the set of features it is focused on, it will reject the fly.

Some fly patterns can actually be more attractive to trout than natural food because they exaggerate the right features and produce more stimulus to the trout than the natural. It is the imitation, or even exaggeration, of the insect's vulnerability that often makes these patterns effective, rather than precise imitation of the insect's anatomy.

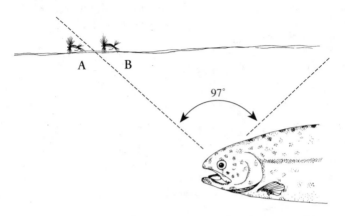

Figure 6-1. *Trout's cone of vision (window). Surface object* B *is visible,* A *is not.*

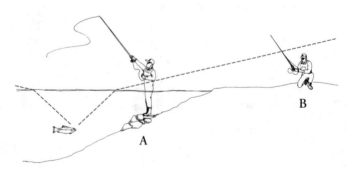

Figure 6-2. *What trout see above and below surface.*
A—*Wading flyfisher visible above water and below.*
B—*Flyfisher kneeling on bank is not visible.*

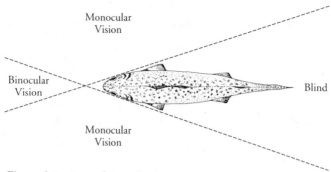

Figure 6-3. *Areas of vision for trout.*

Approaching Trout

Let not our looks put on our purposes.
    Julius Caesar

What Trout See

Trout have incredibly sharp eyesight and see well in low light.
They see everything under the water, limited only by obstructions
and water clarity. But they have a restricted view of anything above
the water's surface (like your dry fly or you) due to refraction. This
is called the trout's "window." It is a cone of vision that is about
97 degrees wide, regardless of the depth or orientation of the fish.
This means that, in theory, a trout can see a surface object that is
about as far in front of it as the trout is deep. A trout 3 feet deep
can see a surface object that is a little more than three feet away in
any direction. A trout 3 inches deep can only see a surface object
a little more than 3 inches away.

Through the window the trout can only see the top portion of objects that are significantly above the surface—like flyfishers—and what they see is distorted.

While much has been written about the trout's window—accompanied by text-book pictures of refracted light rays and perfectly calm water—much of it is misleading. Anything that pierces the surface, deforms it, or creates bubbles is visible to the trout. The feet of drifting duns make little dimples of light that are visible under water well before the wings of the dun are perceived through the window. Also, when the surface of the water is riffled or choppy, its bloody hard to see anything through it clearly.

Trout have binocular vision (with good depth perception) in a narrow area, and monocular vision in a wide area. There is only a small area where they can see nothing.

What Trout Hear, Feel, and Smell

There are other ways besides vision by which a trout can detect your presence. They can hear you if you are wading in a splashy fashion, clanking a wading staff on the bottom, rolling boulders against one another, and any number of other things that make sound waves in the water.

They can also feel your presence from pressure differences caused by unusual wave patterns that you might make while wading. And they can probably even smell you or taste differences in the water due to your presence.

Guidelines for Approaching Trout

Stay out of the water, if possible.

Cast from a kneeling position when possible, either on the bank, or even in the water if it is shallow.

Scrunch down to make yourself lower.

Use trees and brush for cover.

Put rough, broken water between you and the fish. This will help hide you from view.

Avoid casting shadows—you, your rod arm, your rod, your fly line—over the trout's field of view. Know the position of the sun and where your shadow is.

Be careful in shallow areas, like the inlet areas of lakes; trout can be especially wary there.

Clear, slow water gives trout a good view of you and your movements; be especially careful in these waters.

You can approach nearer to a shallow lying trout than to a deep holding one.

Standing or kneeling quietly for 5 minutes before you start casting can make a big difference. It can take at least that long for trout to settle down after your arrival.

Clothing Guidelines

Some people actually wear camouflage clothing and camouflage grease paint on their faces. They catch a lot of fish. Of course, if you go to the river dressed like a commando and don't catch fish you will look like an idiot; perhaps this is a good incentive.

Match the background. Trout (we believe) are color blind except at close range, so match the intensity of the reflected light of the background. Think of yourself and the background as a black-and-white photograph: you want to be a shade of gray that matches the background's shade of gray. Usually this means dark colors such as greens, browns, or blues. Even in a desert the riparian zone is your background, and it is usually green, even though ten feet from the water it may be all tan grass and sand. Clothing in camouflage patterns is good because it breaks up your outline.

Avoid light reflecting objects. Keep shiny metal forceps, nippers, and other light-catchers out of sight. Mirrored sunglasses? Forget 'em!

No bright clothing. Leave your day-glo pink jacket at home. Anything big and bright is unusual to a fish—and therefore a threat. (A new theory for biologists to investigate: an appreciation of fashion exists only at the top of the food chain.)

Presenting

You must cast closer to a shallow fish than to a deep one. Shallow fish are usually focused on the surface close in front of them. Due to this focus and the window, a shallow fish won't see a fly that is too far away.

Both under-surface flies and flies that significantly pierce the surface (spinners and some emerger patterns) are more easily seen from a distance than are traditional dry flies. Switching from a dry fly to a sub-surface emerger can make all the difference if the fish are close to the surface, because they can see the fly coming from farther away.

A Few Other Ways You Can Scare Trout

Spook small fish. Small fish are usually in the top water or in shallow water. Spook them, and they head past the bigger fish on their way to deeper water. The big fish now know there is a predator in the area and will also go down.

Cause a sudden flight of frightened ducks or other water birds.

Walk heavily on the bank over undercuts.

Make sudden, fast movements. These are the movements of a predator and trout are very alert to them.

Walk clumsily across a boulder field that extends from the bank into the water. Banging two rocks together above the water can be transmitted into the water.

Make lots of splashes while wading.

Wade in quiet water so that a bow wave is pushed in front of you.

Stir up mud and silt so it drifts downstream to the trout. Trout know that means something large and possibly predatory is upstream.

The Best Teacher You'll Have

Most fisherman scare more fish in a week than they see in a year. Take a lesson from the Great Blue Heron:

Blend into the background.

Move slowly and carefully, without disturbing the water.

Wait till you locate your fish (visually or see a rise), then go for it.

Wading

Have you a mind to sink?
  The Tempest

General Guidelines

Hip boots tempt you into water that is too deep. They fill easily with water and are hard to get off in an emergency.

Water is always deeper than you think.

Rocks are always more slippery than you think.

When wading through weed beds, you never know how deep the water is, but it is always deeper than you think. Weeds often grow in soft silt, so though it may look two feet deep, but by the time you get past the weeds and sink into the mud it may be four or five feet deep. Is any rising fish worth being stuck in mud with water up to your chin?

Wear a belt around the outside of your waders so they will not fill as fast if you fall in. This is not as necessary if you have neoprene waders. However, if you are float-tubing a lake, a belt is a good idea even with neoprene waders since they will fill with water if given enough time. Think about how far you are from shore and how far you would have to swim if your tube sprung a leak—then you might think about what a good idea a belt would be.

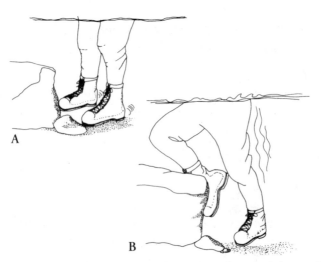

Figure 6-4. A—*Small steps close to bottom let you keep your balance and feel for rocks and holes.*
B—*Large, high steps set you up to stumble.*

Use a wading staff: an old ski pole, a sturdy rake handle, or one of those nifty folding ones from the fly shop. You are less likely to fall in, and even if you don't sink, falling in scares the fish. Don't clank the staff along the bottom—fish hear it. A rubber crutch tip can make your staff quieter.

Long underwear is more comfortable than jeans under your waders. Polypropylene and similar synthetics are good because they are warm, form-fitting, and wick away perspiration.

Before moving a foot, make sure the other foot is securely placed. Keep your feet close to the bottom to avoid stumbling on rocks or stepping in holes. Take small, slow steps, and feel ahead with your feet.

Move slowly and quietly so as not to disturb the fish. Try not to crunch rocks as you move—fish can hear you coming.

Move sideways to the current—you are more stable.

Don't cross your feet—this is an unstable position.

Be especially careful turning around. The most unstable position is when your back is to the current; a heavy current could buckle your knees and set you adrift.

Climbing in or out of the water from a log can be dangerous because they can be slippery and unstable. Look for something solid instead.

Its always easier to move downstream in fast water than upstream. When wading downstream think, "Can I get back upstream again?"

Look carefully when you wade. There might be a fish in your path. If you flush one out, don't worry about it. Come back later and fish that spot. He'll probably be back.

Don't wade through spawning beds.

Walking backwards while wading is a really bad idea.

Figure 6-5. *Don't use a float tube in a river.*

If You Fall in and are Carried Downstream

It would be best to read this section before you fall in: you might not have the presence of mind to pull the book out and read it while being swept through Devil's Washboard rapids.

Don't panic

Face downstream, on your back with your knees pulled up—use your feet to cushion against rocks, and your arms to maneuver.

Don't let yourself be swept onto the upstream side of a large rock or log—you could be pinned to it by the current.

Don't stick a foot between two rocks where it might get wedged.

Grab an overhanging branch, if possible, and swing yourself up onto shore.

When in calmer water, swim for shore.

Leader

Purpose of Leader

Your leader is one of the most important pieces of fly fishing equipment you own. Using the correct leader enables you to:

Smoothly transfer the momentum of the fly line to your fly so it is possible to deliver the fly to the water with accuracy and stealth.

Have the fly move naturally in subtle nuances of current.

Separate the highly visible fly line from the fly. Make no mistake: trout know your leader is there. But the thin leader is less startling to trout than your thick fly line.

Leader Taper

Commercial leaders will become dis-proportioned as you tie on new flies or adjust tippet sizes. Use a leader micrometer (available at fly shops for a modest fee) to check the leader diameter. Then add new sections using blood knots and tippet material.

Figure 6-6 shows leader formulas for four nine foot leaders. These can be used as a guide for either tying your own leaders or for re-building commercial leaders. For longer or shorter leaders the proportions are the same.

9' 3X		9' 4X	
Diameter	Length	Diameter	Length
.021	28"	.021	28"
.019	22"	.019	22"
.017	8"	.017	8"
.015	8"	.015	8"
.013	8"	.013	8"
.011	8"	.011	8"
.009	10"	.009	10"
.008	25"	.007	25"

9' 5X		9' 6X	
Diameter	Length	Diameter	Length
.021	27"	.021	27"
.019	21"	.019	21"
.017	8"	.017	8"
.015	8"	.015	8"
.013	8"	.013	8"
.011	6"	.011	6"
.009	6"	.009	6"
.007	8"	.007	8"
.006	25"	.005	25"

Figure 6-6. *Leader formulas for four nine foot leaders.*

Use a blood knot to join leader sections of the same diameter, or one or two "X" sizes difference. If there are more than two X sizes difference between the sections, use a surgeon's knot.

Always use at least 18" of knot-free tippet.

Attach 18" of stiff leader butt material to your fly line, then tie new leaders onto this section. This will save you from having to tie a new nail knot each time you replace the entire leader.

Some commercial leaders come with butt sections and/or tippet sections that are too short, so you might want to do some adjusting.

When fishing clear, spring creeks or similarly demanding water, you may want to significantly increase the length of the tippet section.

When fishing with a four foot leader, as when using wet flies on a sinking or sink-tip line, leader taper becomes less important and you can get by with only three or four different leader diameters. But you should still maintain 12-18 inches of knot-free tippet.

If you are fishing a very heavily weighted fly, like a girdlebug, on a floating line, leader taper is also of less importance because of the way you are casting.

Choosing a Tippet Size

Tippet sizes are listed by "X" size. The "X" size is determined by subtracting the diameter, in thousandths of an inch, from 11. Thus 0X is .011 inches thick, 5X is .006 inches thick, and so on.

A useful rule of thumb is to choose a tippet "X" size that is equal to the fly size (in equivalent dry fly hook size) divided by 3. So if you are casting a size 12 dry fly, a 4X tippet is a good starting point, and a size 18 fly would use a 6X tippet.

However, this rule of thumb is just a starting point. Several factors can cause you to modify it. These include:

Bigger, more active fish might require a stronger tippet.

Clear water and spooky fish might dictate a thinner tippet.

Tricky currents that make your fly want to wiggle in the flow may mean you need a limper, thinner tippet.

Leader Length

For general use on dry lines, 9 feet is a good length.

For full-sinking and sink-tip lines, use a short leader—about 4 feet—so the fly stays down with the line.

When casting a floating line from brushy areas, a seven foot leader will be easier to handle.

On extremely clear water, such as spring creeks, go for 12 feet and the thinnest tippet you can get away with. Sometimes you need even more leader; 18 feet may be needed in very clear lakes with wary fish.

More Tippet Tips

To straighten your tippet, use a piece of India rubber (often sold in fly stores) or a piece of old inner tube. Hold it between your fingers with the leader in the middle and run it down the last few feet of leader.

If your tippet is kinking up and you can't straighten it, replace it.

"Mud" or some similar material (available in fly shops) can be used to sink the last few inches of tippet when presenting dry flies. This is often necessary with cautious fish, especially in sunny conditions.

Knots are breaking points, and they are also big and catch the light, which can spook fish. There comes a time when you need to catch fish and to stop trying to save a buck. Replace the leader when it has too many knots.

Don't put line dressing on the leader when fishing in rivers. This creates additional drag by having the leader in the surface film.

Mending and Other Ways of Dealing with Drag

All the more it seeks to hide itself, the bigger bulk it shows.
The Tempest

Mending

All flowing water has different "speed zones" of current. Even in an unbroken, smooth river the current will be slower on the sides and bottom. When portions of your fly line or leader cross currents of differing speeds, the line will bow downstream and pull upon your fly, causing it to move in an unnatural manner. This is known as "drag," and trout have the annoying habit of ignoring a dragging fly when they see one.

Drag is a problem for both wet and dry flies. Wet flies and nymphs are acted upon by currents which vary in velocity from top to bottom as well as currents which vary across the stream width. Drag also occurs in lakes, where it is caused by wind, boat movement, and lake currents.

"Mending" is the process of moving the drifting fly line and leader so as to delay the effects of drag. Mends can be either upstream or downstream. Some important points about mending:

The key is not to move the fly as you mend the line.

Mending is done with more of a lifting and moving motion than a casting motion.

You cannot mend a line that is under the water. A well dressed line will be easier to mend since less of it will be submerged.

Do not dress the leader in rivers, as this actually increases drag.

See figure 6-7 on the following page for an illustration of mending a cast to alleviate drag.

Other Ways of Dealing with Drag

Before casting, study the current. Then position yourself so that your cast covers as few speed zones as possible.

Cast as little line as possible. Position yourself as close to the trout as you can. See pages 173-177 for guidelines on approaching trout.

Use the slack cast to put slack into the line and leader and give you a few precious seconds of drag-free drift (see page 192).

Use the reach cast to put a built-in mend into your cast. (See page 192).

Cast straight downwind, or quarter your cast 45 degrees to the wind, and mend line upwind when fishing lakes on windy days from a float tube or an unanchored boat. If you are anchored, an upwind cast may be better so that the fly will drift back to you.

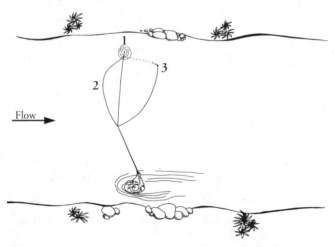

Figure 6-7. *Mending to delay drag. Cast (1), then mend (2) to get a drag free drift (3).*

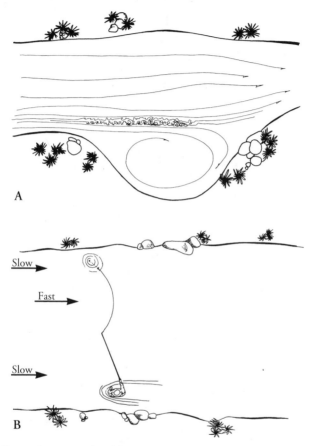

Figure 6-8. *Examples of drag.*
A—*Water on the outside of a back eddy has many micro-eddies; drag-free drift is very difficult to achieve.*
B—*Different speed zones in a smooth flow create a belly in the line, causing the fly to drag.*

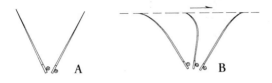

Figure 6-9. *Rod motion and casting arcs.*
    A—Basic casting arc   *C—Convex arc*
    B—Level casting arc   *D—Concave arc*

Don't leave your fly on the water too long. If it starts to drag, pick up and cast again. Several casts with short drifts can be more effective than fewer casts with long drifts that start to drag. However, when you pick up, make sure your fly has drifted beyond the trout's window of vision. Otherwise you risk spooking the fish.

Recognize that sometimes you can't avoid drag, and there are some spots you just can't fish. This is often true of certain parts of backeddies (usually the part with the biggest fish). Give it a few tries, then move on to other water.

Casting Problems and Special Situations

Past hope, past cure, past help.
   Romeo and Juliet

Overhead Cast

This cast is your bread-and-butter basic cast. Nearly all basic casting problems are caused by:

Breaking the wrist, which causes too wide a casting arc.

Too early application of power on the forward stroke.

Too short a casting arc.

Not stopping the rod on either the backcast or the forward cast.

Here's a quick review of casting basics and terminology that apply to these problems:

   Rod motion for most casts is between 11 o'clock and 1 o'clock . This is called the casting arc. The casting arc can start at any reasonable "clock" position, but generally needs to cover only two "hours."

   A convex casting arc, where the tip of the rod is highest in the middle of the stroke, causes a very wide casting loop, or no loop at all. Sometimes a wide loop is desirable, however it can mean loss of distance and accuracy. In extreme cases it can mean the line, leader, and fly all end up in a pile on the water.

Figure 6-10. *Imagine your rod is a fork with mashed potatoes on the tip.*

Breaking the wrist usually causes a convex casting arc.

A too wide casting arc usually causes a convex casting arc.

The dynamics of the cast are to accelerate to a stop on both your backward and forward strokes. Think of it this way: if you had mashed potatoes on a fork and you wanted to fling it across the room at someone, you couldn't do it if you moved the fork too quickly when you first started. You would need to start the fork slowly, accelerate it, then stop it suddenly. The mashed potatoes would fly across the room and splat on something (or somebody). The dynamics of fly casting are the same as for mashed potatoes.

A wide casting loop results in a softer delivery of the fly. It also means you can't cast as far. Long, thin leaders often need a wide loop for proper delivery of the fly. The conventional wisdom is that wide loops are "bad casting." However, there are times when a wide casting loop is needed for proper presentation.

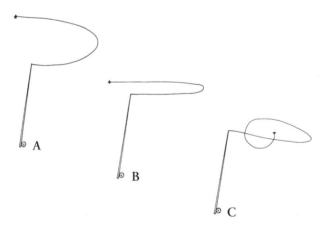

Figure 6-11. *Casting loops.*   A—*Wide*   B—*Narrow*   C—*Tailing*

Other Subjects

Tailing loops, where the leader falls back on the line, are usually caused by applying power too soon in the forward stroke. See the mashed potatoes analogy above. Tailing loops result in knots in the leader and in the leader getting tangled in the fly line.

Casting a Heavy Fly

You can't cast a heavy fly like a girdlebug the same way you cast a size 20 midge. You have a rock on a string, and different techniques are needed.

In most cases you will be in a river casting upstream. Let the fly, leader, and line hang straight below you in the current. Then lift the rod so most of the line breaks free of the water; the fly will still be in the water, but near the surface. Pause briefly, then cast forward. The rod should travel in a wide, convex arc. The cast should be relatively slow, with the rod brought right down to the water and pointing straight at where you want the cast to go. You want the fly and leader to be in a straight line with the current direction, so mend the line if necessary. If you have a problem with accuracy, it may be caused by too fast a cast, which makes the fly line shock against the rod and bounce in a different direction. There is little or no false casting with this technique.

Figure 6-12. *Casting a heavily-weighted fly.*
With line and fly hanging straight below you in the current (1), lift the rod and pause briefly (2). Rod travels in wide, convex arc (3).

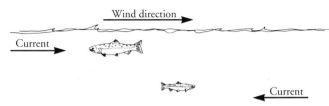

Figure 6-13. *Windy day on a lake. Wind produces a subsurface current. Cast across the wind to give trout a broadside look at your fly.*

Roll Cast

When you have an obstacle behind you, the roll cast may be the only cast you can make. With the line resting straight on the water in front of you, bring the rod to a vertical position so line hangs down from the rod tip at your shoulder. Your rod hand should be high. Then power the rod down to a horizontal position like you were driving a nail with a hammer.

Reach Cast

Do a normal overhead cast, but as the fly is being delivered, reach to the side (usually upstream) with your casting arm. A reach cast is really a cast with a built-in mend.

Slack Cast

As the fly is being delivered, wiggle the rod tip back and forth. The line will land on the water in snake-like curves. The current can pull out the slack in the line without dragging the fly too much.

Pickups

The pickup is how you get the fly and line off the water at the end of one cast as you prepare for the next. Poor pickups put down more fish than most anglers realize. Your fly needs to leave the water gracefully and with as little disturbance to the water as possible. One way to achieve this with a dry fly is to give a quick little roll cast as the start of your next cast. This breaks the fly and line free from the water. Once it is free, begin your normal cast.

Placing Your Casts

Before you cast, think about where the big fish are. Don't spook the big fish by casting over them and "lining" them. You also scare big fish by hooking a smaller fish and then dragging it—splashing and flailing—through prime holding water.

Once you have resolved the "big fish" issue, cast so as to cover the nearest desirable fish first without putting your fly line over other fish.

When fishing with a count-down-and-retrieve tactic in lakes, casts near reefs and weed beds should be nearly parallel to them. This way your fly will remain longer in the best water. Similarly, casts along a floating log should be almost parallel to the log.

In lakes on windy days, there will be a current just under the surface flowing in the direction of the wind. Slightly deeper, there will be a current in the opposite direction. This means that fish near the surface will either have their heads into the wind (if they are higher), or their tails (if they are lower). If you are using a count-down-and-retrieve presentation in the top few feet of water, place your casts across the wind. This will present the trout with a broadside view of your fly and increase the chances of a take.

If fish are not visible, cover the good water in a consistent manner. If you think the fish are lying deep, then the space between casts should vary with water clarity—the clearer the water the more space you can put between casts.

Odds and Ends

Using a dropper to fish two flies. Figure 6-14 shows how to rig up a dropper so you can fish two flies at once.

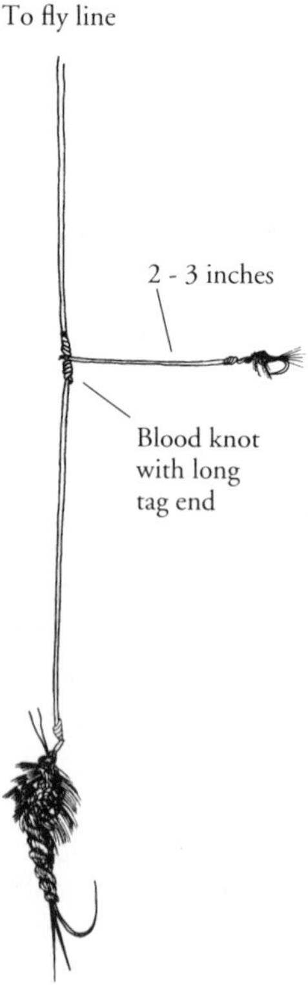

To fly line

2 - 3 inches

Blood knot
with long
tag end

Figure 6-14. *Dropper rig*

Trolling from a float tube. Cast out your line and let it sink to the proper depth. Kick with your feet to achieve the proper speed. Hold your rod out to the side so you are not passing directly over the fish with your tube.

To troll and retrieve, cast and let the fly sink to the proper depth, then kick very slowly while retrieving. This lets you cover more water and impart a more interesting action to the fly.

Long retrieves from a float tube. This is useful when fishing a sinking line near the bottom. Cast as far as you can. While the fly and line are sinking, back pedal in the float tube while letting out more line. Go all the way into your backing, then start retrieving. You should get a long retrieve at a consistent depth.

Stretching line. When casting and retrieving, your loose fly line will pile up in coils at your feet or on your float tube apron. To avoid tangling, grab the line between your hands and stretch it when you first pull it off the reel. You may need to repeat this after your line has dried a while on the reel.

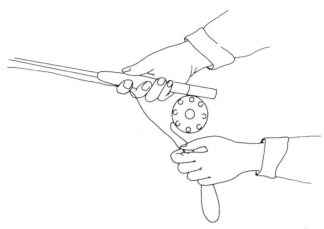

Figure 6-15. *Keeping a tight line. Pull the fly line through the index finger of your rod hand*

Tight line. You will have more consistent success if you minimize the slack line between you and the fish. With a tight line, you'll be able to strike quickly enough to hook a fish. On an upstream cast, this means pulling in the slack as the line drifts down to you. Be careful not to disturb the fly as you do this. You need to keep a balance between having enough slack to avoid drag, and keeping the line tight enough to allow you to strike quickly.

Failure to manage slack line is one of the biggest mistakes beginning flyfishers make. Keep your index finger of your rod hand on the line, then pull in slack from behind it.

Drying flies. Flies can be dried out somewhat with repeated false casts. This is a good thing for dry flies since you want them to float, but a bad thing for nymphs that you want to sink. There are commercial preparations for drying flies that work well, especially after the fly has been slimed by a hooked fish.

Short strikes. Fish that hit a sunken fly on the retrieve but don't get hooked can sometimes be brought back by stopping the retrieve briefly, then beginning again.

Keep your rod low! Keeping your rod tip just above the water minimizes slack line, and helps you concentrate on keeping the rod—and fly—still.

Keep your rod high! Holding your casting arm high, with the rod parallel to the water, can keep the line from getting tangled in drag-producing current between you and the fly. Whether you keep your rod high or low will depend on the situation you are facing at the moment.

Barbless hooks. Barbless hooks penetrate faster, and therefore hook fish more quickly. They hold the fish just as well as barbed hooks. They are more easily removed from fish, as well from your clothes and various parts of your body.

Figure 6-16. A—*Rod low to minimize slack and movement*
B—*Rod high to avoid drag*

Other Subjects

Sharpening hooks. Hooks quickly grow dull with use, and many hooks are not sharp enough even when new. Sharp, barbless hooks penetrate easily and will improve your chances of securely hooking trout. If you are getting hits to your fly, but the trout don't stay on very long, a dull hook could be the culprit.

To sharpen a hook, use a hook file to fashion a triangular point: flat on the bottom, angled on the sides. When sharp, the hook will stick as you brush it across your thumbnail. Test for sharpness each time you tie on a fly, and check it frequently, especially if you are fishing sunken flies over a rocky bottom.

Dressing the line. Floating line should be dressed at least once a day to help it cast well, as well as to keep the line freer of the water for a more drag-free drift and easier mending. To do a really good job, on the day before you go fishing:

1. Strip the line off the reel.

2. Wash it in mildly soapy water, then rinse well.

3. Dry it with a towel.

4. Apply line dressing sparingly to somewhat more line than your longest casting distance.

5. Allow dressing to dry. Drying time varies with different products. It may take two or three hours.

6. Buff the dressing with a clean towel. Then buff it again.

7. Reel line back onto reel.

No Fish? What to do When Nothing Works

Alas, poor fool, how they have baffled thee.
Twelfth Night

If Fish are Rising and You Get No Response

Use a pattern that matches the available insects and not an attractor pattern.

Check the order of the hatching insects: don't fish a caddis pattern in a mayfly hatch!

Imitate a different POV.

Check size. Get a sample of the hatch and measure it; it's easy to be one hook size too big.

Check color. Get a sample of the hatch and examine with a hand lens and flashlight; color is hard to judge from a distance, so get up close.

Use a fly with less hackle, or trim some of the hackle off the pattern you are using; use the minimum hackle necessary to float the fly.

Go to a finer tippet.

Sink the last few inches of tippet with "mud".

Straighten the tippet.

Lengthen the leader. Sometimes you need more space between the line and the leader. Twelve feet may be necessary, or even 15 feet or 18 feet. Yes, long leaders are a pain to cast.

Watch for drag. If the current is tricky you may need to change casting position, to cast shorter, to use a finer tippet, or to fish different water. Sometimes drag problems can't be solved; recognize when you're snookered and move on.

Check for a multiple hatch. Small, dark insects may be masked by a hatch of larger, lighter insects, but the trout are taking the dark ones that are hard to see; also, they may be taking spinners, which are even harder to see.

Switch to a nymph or other wet fly if you are fishing a dry. Often trout are not as fussy about a sub-surface fly as a dry, and they can see a sub-surface fly from farther away than a dry.

Stop casting for 5 minutes and let the fish adjust to your presence. Hide yourself, if possible.

Seek out wind-riffled water. If the air is very still and the water is glassy calm, the fish can see everything with absolute clarity. Fishing either surface or subsurface flies in these conditions can be unproductive. Look for water that has a little wind-riffle on it and fish there. A nymph may be more effective there than a dry.

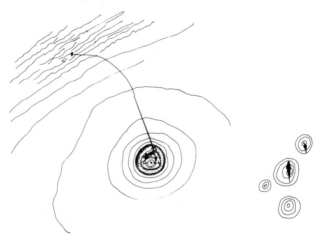

Figure 6-17. *Seeking wind-riffled water on a lake.*

Are there a lot of people fishing where you are? If the fish have been flogged for hours, or even days—as a concentration of large feeding fish often will be—get away from the crowd. You have a better chance fishing over fewer—but less wary—fish.

Fish a different style of fly. If everyone else is fishing Hare's Ear nymphs, try a Pheasant Tail. Or invent a new one. In areas with heavy fishing pressure, the fish get educated about fake flies, so give them something they haven't seen.

Wade out into the middle of the fish and take a bug sample with your nymph net. Then spend 15 minutes figuring out what to do next; this gives the trout time to settle down again after you've traumatized them. This probably will not work with large trout, who are more wary. And, unless you want to be lynched, make sure you are the only person on the water.

No Surface Activity, No Fish Seen

In Rivers:

Try a double nymph rig. Use two different sizes.

Change the kind of water you're fishing. Find out what type of water receptive fish are in (fast, slow, riffles, backeddies, etc.).

Pick good water and fish it. Sometimes the feeding activity is so subtle you can't see it. Slow down and fish the water anyway. After a while you may see activity that you missed, or maybe the fish were just sitting quietly waiting for a bug to drift down.

In Lakes:

Try different parts of the lake, especially if you are in a boat or float tube. Troll around until you find where fish are.

Experiment with different retrieves at different depths while using a general pattern like a wooly bugger or leech.

Try different colors. Sometimes the difference between a brown leech and a black leech is profound.

Copy the retrieve of someone who is catching fish.

Nothing Works:

Ask somebody who is catching fish. They may be delighted to tell you the secret of the day.

Observe. Put down the rod and watch what's happening. You may see activity you missed because you were focused too narrowly. Take insect samples, measure the water depth, check out the birds.

Practice casting.

Enjoy the out-of-doors. It is not necessary to catch fish to have fun. Read a book, take a picture, take a hike, take a snooze.

Wait patiently for it to get better. Sometimes when there are three kinds of midges, several caddis species, a few mayfly spinners, an abundance of scuds and leeches—all active at the same time and the fish could be taking any stage of any of them at any depth, and the water is very clear and has had a lot of fishing pressure—you just may not figure out how to catch the fish. Contemplate more answerable questions, like: can global hunger be ended? Where does evil originate? Can bait fisherman be trained not to litter? There's more to fishing than catching fish; enjoy the total experience.

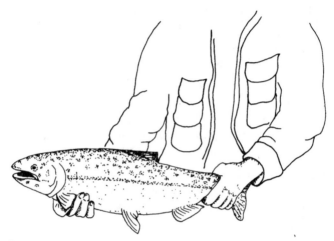

Figure 6-18. *Holding a fish prior to release.*

Releasing Fish

The quality of mercy is not strained.
    The Merchant of Venice

Wild fish are an irreplaceable natural resource. Releasing them allows their unique genetic traits to be perpetuated for the enjoyment of all. Fish over 12" are often the primary wild spawners, so if you are going to keep fish, keep the little ones and let the big ones go.

There are many reasons for releasing fish, even hatchery fish. Before killing a trout, ask yourself: do I really need to eat this guy? Wouldn't it be great if someone else could enjoy catching this fish, too? Is my ego so fragile that I have to take this fish home as proof that I'm smarter than a pea-brained salmonid? There is more pleasure in catching trout than in eating them.

How to Release fish Unharmed

Use barbless hooks.

Don't play the fish too long, especially during, just before, or just after the spawning season.

Wet your hands before handling fish.

If the water is warm, avoid touching the fish at all. Leave it in the water and remove the hook with forceps. In warm water, bacteria growth is quick. Handling fish—with wet or dry hands, with or without cotton gloves—removes some of the slime coating that protects fish against bacteria, which is a much bigger problem in warm water than in cold.

Back the hook out carefully with your fingers or forceps.

Don't squeeze the fish.

Don't hold it by the mouth.

Don't put your fingers in its gills.

Don't bang it on the rocks.

If the fish is hooked any deeper than the lips, cut your leader. Do this immediately; don't fiddle with it. The fly will soon work itself out without harm to the fish.

Don't get the fish all tangled up in your net, especially the gills.

It is best never to remove the trout from the water. If you must take it out for a photo, keep it out of water for as little time as possible.

If you need to hold the fish, as for a photo, grasp it in front of the tail with one hand, and support the head with the other. Your grip will be more sure if you have a cotton glove on the grasping hand, or use a handkerchief.

Figure 6-19. *Reviving a trout in fast water. Use your leg to break the current.*

To revive a tired fish, grasp it in front of the tail (as described above) and move it back and forth in the water so its gills are working; don't let go the first time the fish tries to escape, but wait for the second time. In rivers, you can help the fish by holding it downstream from your leg. This way your leg will break the current for the fish.

Never just drop a fish into fast water. If they start to tumble in the current they may not regain their equilibrium, and will suffocate.

What Did You Catch?

We did keep time, sir, in our catches.
Twelfth Night

Rainbow Trout

Numerous spots on head

Dark spots, light background

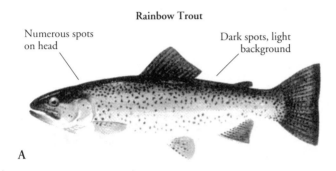

A

Cutthroat Trout

Few spots on head

Dark spots, light background

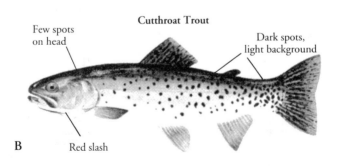

B

Red slash

Figure 6-20. A—*Rainbow Trout* B—*Cutthroat Trout*

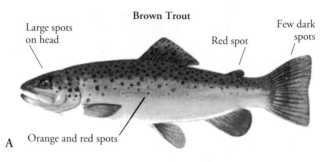

Brown Trout

Large spots on head

Red spot

Few dark spots

Orange and red spots

A

Brook Trout

Worm-like markings

Light spots, dark background

Red spots

Dark and light edge on fins

B

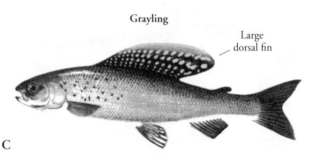

Grayling

Large dorsal fin

C

Figure 6-21. A—*Brown Trout*   B—*Brook Trout*   C—*Grayling*

Mountain Whitefish

Small mouth,
no teeth

Figure 6-22. *Mountain Whitefish*

Knots

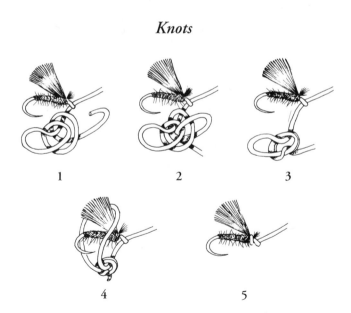

1

2

3

4

5

Figure 6-23. *Double Turle Knot. Use for small flies (size 10 or smaller).*

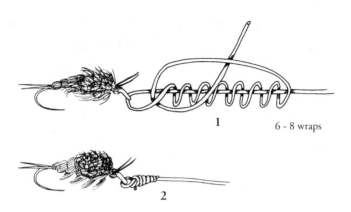

Figure 6-24. *Improved Clinch Knot. Use for large flies, streamers.*

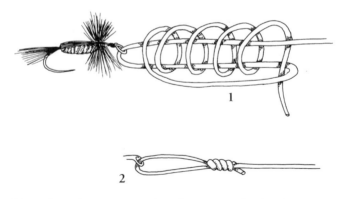

Figure 6-25. *Duncan Loop. Gives freer action to flies, keeps knot away from head of small flies, so fly still looks small!*

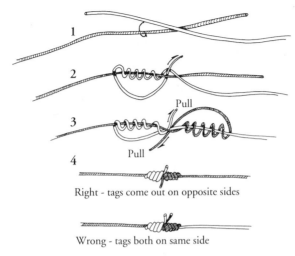

Figure 6-26. *Blood Knot.   Use to join together two sections of leader which differ in diameter by no more than 2 "X" sizes.*

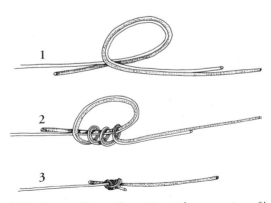

Figure 6-27. *Surgeons Knot.   Use to join together two sections of leader, especially when they differ in diameter by greater than 2 "X" sizes.*

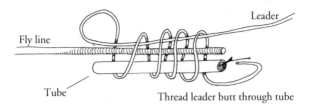

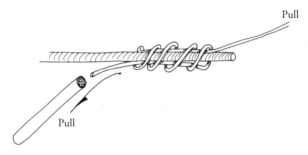

Figure 6-28. *Tube Knot or Nail Knot.   Use to join fly line to leader butt. This illustration uses a tube to simplify the tie, but a nail will work in its place. After wrapping the leader, remove the nail and put the tag end through the space the nail occupied.*

Ethics and Etiquette

Fly fishing, more than any other method of fishing, stresses being in harmony with your environment. The fly fishing angler is an observant participant in an entire ecosystem of water, plants, trees, birds, insects, fish of all species, people, and even soil and rocks. All are intricately linked together. We each have a responsibility to educate ourselves about the issues concerning this ecosystem, and to work for its improvement and preservation.

The best guide for streamside etiquette is the Golden Rule: Do unto others as you would have them do unto you.

If someone is fishing an area near where you want to fish, ask if you will disturb them. If they are sitting, and not fishing, they may be resting the water or waiting for the light to change. In either case, ask before you fish.

Don't be a hole hog — don't hog the good water all day long. Give someone else a chance.

If you are fishing from a boat, give bank anglers a wide berth. Watch where they are casting to and give them lots of space. If you aren't sure where they are fishing, ask so you can avoid the place. When you are in a boat, you have access to more water than bank anglers, so give them a break.

Check the local fishing regulations and follow them.

Don't pee in the lake or river. Do it at least 20 feet from shore.

Bury feces. With your boot or a stick, dig a 6" deep hole at least 150 feet from the water, and cover it up when you're done.

Don't litter. You packed it in, you can pack it out. This includes leader packages and old leaders. Don't throw cigarette butts in the water or in the bushes.

Leave an area looking better than you found it. If you see trash, old cans, or bottles, pick them up and dispose of them. This is a contagious habit. Once you start doing it, many others will follow your example.

Each river or lake can have its own code of conduct and etiquette. Be sensitive to this.

Be extremely careful with fires.

Enjoy your fishing, and share your enjoyment with others. Share insights, information, even flies with other anglers.

Glossary

Active presentation. Moving the fly through line action, such as a retrieve or twitch. Contrast with "dead drift."

Attractor fly. A fly pattern that does not imitate a particular insect or other trout food, but is still attractive to trout, sometimes.

Back eddy. A portion of the river where the shape of the river bank causes the current next to the shore to loop in a circle.

Behavioral drift. Individuals of some insect species release themselves from the river bottom and drift downstream several yards. This usually occurs at predictable times of the day, most often dawn and dusk. The nymphs are vulnerable to trout at this time.

Caddisfly. See pages 128-131.

Cascade. A section of river with falls and drops.

Catastrophic drift. Nymphs or larva that are dislodged and set adrift for reasons beyond their instinctual desires.

Cranefly. An insect of the family Tipulidae; see pages 125-126.

Chironomid. Usually a midge; a member of the family Chironomidae; see pages 125-126.

Cripple. An emerging insect that is stuck in its pupal or nymphal case and cannot get out. Similar to the hatching POV.

Cut bank. Where the water has worked its way under the river bank or lake shore, forming overhead cover for trout.

Damselfly. See pages 127-128.

Dapping. Tapping the water surface with a dangling fly. See page 106.

Dead drift. A drag-free drift of the fly, either dry or wet. See pages 185-188.

Diptera. The insect order that includes midges. See pages 125-126.

Downstream. In a river, where the water is going to.

Downwing. Sometimes used to describe aquatic insects that are not mayflies. Also used to describe a fly pattern with the wing parallel to the body. Many wet fly patterns, including those that represent some emerging mayflies, are downwing patterns.

Drag. Unnatural fly movement caused by current pulling the fly line. See pages 185-188.

Dragonfly. See pages 127-128.

Drainage lake. A lake whose water comes from an inlet stream.

Dropper. An additional fly attached above the leader end. See page 194.

Dry fly. A fly that is designed to stay above the surface of the water, thus imitating many phases of adult insect behavior.

Dun. The first adult stage of mayflies. Duns will molt once more into spinners. Same as "Subimago."

Emerger. An insect in transition to adult from nymph or pupa.

Ephemeroptera. The insect order of mayflies. See pages 120-124.

False cast. Casting that does not put the fly on the water.

Family. Part of the scientific classification system. See pages 90-91.

Flat. A section of river with slow current and few obstructions.

Floatant. A material, generally silicon-based, that you put on your fly to make it shed water and float better. Also used on fly line.

Floating line. Fly line designed to float on the water surface.

Floating nymph. Emerging mayfly nymph that has come to the underside of the surface film preparatory to emerging as an adult.

Foam line. Turbulent water generates foam, which may be concentrated by the current into a narrow line.

Genera. Plural of genus.

Generic fly. A fly whose appearance is general enough that it represents several types of insects, as long as the trout aren't too fussy. The Adams is a generic dry fly; the Hare's Ear is a generic nymph.

Genus. Part of the scientific classification system. See pages 90-91.

Gillie. In Scotland and Ireland, a fishing guide. See Chapter 1. Alternate spellings include "gilly" and "ghillie."

Hackle. The feathers on a fly. Generally refers to the stiff feathers that make dry flies sit up on the surface of the water.

Hair wing. A fly pattern where the wing is made from hair, typically deer or elk hair. Hair wing patterns float well in rough water.

Helgrammite. Properly speaking, helgrammites are the larvae of dobsonflies. Bait fishermen refer to any large underwater insect as a "helgrammite." See Rule 2 in Chapter 1. The real helgrammite can bite, so handle with care.

Imago. See "Spinner."

Imitator fly. A fly pattern that intentionally mimics a particular insect. See pages 91-97.

Instar. The stage of life of an insect between two molts. See "Molt."

Intermediate line. A fly line that slowly sinks in the water. Often useful in lakes for fishing flies near the surface.

Lake. In this book, a lake is a large section of still water. Portions of some rivers require techniques normally used on lakes.

Larva. The primary form of insects with complete metamorphosis, such as caddisflies and midges. Plural is "larvae." Larvae can be distinguished from nymphs and pupae by the lack of wing pads.

Leech. A worm-like aquatic critter that swims and is desired by trout. See page 112.

Line dressing. Material applied to the fly line to make it float better and move through the rod guides more easily.

Margin. Very slow moving portions of a river next to the shore.

Mayfly. Member of the Ephemerellidae family. See pages 120-124.

Mend. Adjusting the fly line and/or leader to minimize the effect of drag once its on the water. See pages 185-188.

Meniscus. See "Surface Film."

Midge. A member of the family Chironomidae. See pages 125-126.

Molt. In the insect world, the process of shedding the external skeleton for a new one. Nymphs may molt many times before adulthood, and each stage is called an instar.

Mud. A commercial substance used to help leaders break through the surface tension of the water and sink.

Multiple hatch. When two or more insect species are emerging at the same time. See page 169.

Nymph. The primary underwater form of insects with incomplete metamorphosis (eg. mayflies, stoneflies, damselflies, and dragonflies.)

Nymph net. A device for collecting insects of all stages from the water. See page 135.

Odonata. The insect order of damselflies and dragonflies. See pages 127-128.

Opportunistic feeding. Feeding upon whatever passes. See page 169.

Order. Part of the scientific classification system. See pages 90-91.

Oviposit. The process of laying eggs.

Passive presentation. Presenting the fly without imparting additional action of your own.

Phytoplankton. Plant plankton

Plankton. Microscopic plants or animals; eaten by some insects.

Plecoptera. The insect order of stoneflies. See pages 124-125.

POV. Point of Vulnerability. The predictable times in an insect's lifecycle when it is available to feeding trout. A key concept of this book. See pages 31-39.

Pool. A section of river with almost no current, usually deep.

Pupa. The final underwater form of insects with complete metamorphosis. The pupa rises to the surface or crawls to shore and the adult emerges. Plural is "pupae."

Rapids. A section of river with very fast current and large rocks.

Riffle. A section of river with fast current and a broken surface.

Riparian zone. Land near the water where vegetation grows.

Rise. When a trout takes an insect or fly near or on the surface.

River. In this book, a river is a body of moving water. Portions of some rivers are fished like lakes because the water barely moves, but portions of some lakes—generally inlet and outlet areas—are fished with river techniques.

Run. A section of river with moderate to fast flow and smooth surface.

Scud. A small shrimp-like crustacean that trout eat. See pages 111-112.

Sedge. Another name for a caddisfly.

Seepage lake. A lake whose water comes only from underground springs or rainfall and snow melt.

Selective feeding. Feeding locked on single food type. See page 169.

Shuck. The nymph case from which the dun emerges.

Sinking line. Fly line that is designed to sink in the water. The entire line sinks; see "Sinking tip line" below.

Sinking tip line. Fly line that is designed so the tip (typically the first ten or twenty feet) sinks and the rest floats. The floating portion gives the angler some line control for mending.

Slack line. When an angler casts upstream, and the fly and fly line drift downstream, slack line forms between the angler and the fly. If this slack is not controlled, the angler will not be able to tighten the line when a fish takes the fly, and may not hook the fish.

Species. Part of the scientific classification system. See pages 90-91.

Spinner. The final adult form of mayflies. In this stage the mayfly is sexually mature, mates, and the females lay eggs in the water. Many female spinners die on the water with their wings spread out flat to the sides. Same as "Imago."

Spinner fall. When a large number of spinners fall spent on the water at the same time, trout may feed selectively on them.

Spring. A outflowing of groundwater, possibly occurring subsurface.

Stillborn. An adult insect that did not successfully emerge from its nymphal or pupal case.

Stonefly. See pages 124-125.

Subimago. The first adult stage of mayflies. Same as "Dun."

Surface film. Molecules of water at the surface will adhere to each other and make a "sticky" barrier that is difficult for small emergers to break through from underneath. It also supports adults.

Tailing loop. A casting defect that often results in knots in the leader. See pages 189-191.

Tailout. In rivers, most pools start with a fast riffle or rapids, then a deep pool, and last an increasingly shallow area prior to the next riffle or rapids. This last shallow area is the tailout.

Thermocline. A sudden change in water temperature marking the boundary between masses of water that are not mixing. Lakes often have a thermocline during cooler seasons.

Tippet. The final, thinnest section of leader before the fly.

Trichoptera. The insect order of caddisflies. See pages 128-131.

Turnover (casting). As the cast unrolls onto the water, the fly should "turn over" so that leader, line, and fly all land in a straight line.

Turnover (lakes). In the winter when lakes ice over, the coldest water is at the top and the warmest at the bottom. After the ice melts, the surface water sinks to the bottom, and the bottom water rises to the surface. This process is called "turnover." It repeats in the fall.

Upstream. In a river, where the water is coming from.

Upwing. A mayfly insect, or any fly pattern that has the wing upright and perpendicular to the body. See "Downwing."

Wet fly. A fly that is designed to be fished under the surface of the water. Includes nymphs, emergers, streamers, etc.

Wind knot. A knot in the leader usually caused by tailing loops.

Window. The trout's field of view of the water's surface. See pages 172-174.

Zooplankton. Animal plankton.